CALVIN'S DOCTRINE OF PREDESTINATION

SECOND EDITION

Fred H. Klooster

BAKER BIBLICAL MONOGRAPH

BAKER BOOK HOUSE
Grand Rapids, Michigan

Praise be to the God and Father
of our Lord Jesus Christ
who has blessed us in the heavenly realms
with every spiritual blessing in Christ.

To my students

For he chose us in him
before the creation of the world
to be holy and blameless in his sight.

In love he predestined us
to be adopted as sons through Jesus Christ,
in accordance with his pleasure and will—
to the praise of his glorious grace,
which he has freely given us
in the One he loves.

Ephesians 1:3–6 (NIV)

Contents

Foreword

———

IN THE CURRENT RENASCENCE of Reformation studies, the theology of John Calvin has received a considerable share of attention. Among the elements of his theology that have been closely examined, none is more prominent than his doctrine of predestination. This is hardly surprising, since this doctrine has been a bone of contention during nearly the entire history of the Christian church.

In the present study Dr. Klooster deals anew with this doctrine. He does so in the keen awareness of the problems that have been raised and the theories propounded by recent scholarship concerning Calvin's doctrine of predestination. His main point of reference, however, as is quite proper, is the writing of Calvin himself, and particularly his great systematic work, *Institutes of the Christian Religion.* This lucid presentation will bring clearly to the reader's mind Calvin's solution of various problems involved in the doctrine, as well as those elements that Calvin, on the basis of Scripture, deliberately left unresolved.

Dr. Klooster is professor of systematic theology at Calvin Theological Seminary.

J. H. KROMMINGA
President, Calvin Seminary

Preface to
the Second Edition

————

THIS BRIEF STUDY, first prepared for the 400th anniversary of the publication in 1559 of the definitive edition of John Calvin's *Institutes*, was published in 1961 in the Calvin Theological Seminary Monograph Series. I am pleased that Baker Book House is making it available again in this revised edition.

Since I had them in mind in preparing this summary of Calvin's view of predestination, it is fitting that I now dedicate this study to my students—past, present, and future—at Calvin Seminary. My original aim was to present Calvin's thoughts as fairly and as accurately as possible, and to a large extent this has been done in his own words. Not wishing to intrude upon the summary of Calvin's position, I have relegated my discussion with contemporary authors to the footnotes.

The major revision in this second edition concerns the quotations from Calvin's writings. I am here incorporating translations that were not yet available when the first edition was prepared. To introduce the quotations of Calvin from new and fresh translations, many sentences have had to be recast as well. I hope the entire text has become more readable as a result.

I am indebted to my wife, Leona, and my son, David, for reading the revised manuscript and suggesting many improvements. The competent cooperation of the publishers is also gratefully acknowledged.

List of Abbreviations

OC   Calvin, John. *Opera quae supersunt omnia.* Edited by
Guilielmus Baum, Eduardus Cunitz, and Eduardus
Reuss. 59 vols. *Corpus Reformatorum*, vols. 29–87.
Brunsvigae: Schwetschke, 1863–1900.

OS   Calvin, John. *Opera selecta.* Edited by Petrus Barth
and Guilielmus Niesel. 5 vols. Munich: Kaiser, 1926–
1952.

CHAPTER 1

General Features
of Calvin's Doctrine
# of Predestination

CALVIN'S DOCTRINE of predestination has been the occasion for concern and worry for many people. Many have found that this doctrine led them to fret and struggle, worried that they could never be certain of their salvation. "If God decided long ago whether I would be saved or damned," they say, "what can I do now that will make any difference? How can I know for sure that I am among the elect?" Others consider this doctrine unacceptable for its apparent contradiction of human freedom. Yet, ironically, Calvin himself saw this doctrine as possessing great practical benefit. He insisted that it bears "sweet fruits" for the believer; indeed, only by accepting this Biblical doctrine of predestination can the believer find genuine assurance and comfort in his salvation.

Misunderstanding of Calvin's teaching continues to challenge much of modern Calvin scholarship. "Calvin formerly stirred debate because people agreed or disagreed with his teaching. Recently men have been in disagreement with regard to what his teaching was."[1] This judgment of John T. McNeill accurately reflects the state of Calvin studies[2] since Karl Barth's theology sparked a re-

1. John T. McNeill, *The History and Character of Calvinism*, p. 202.

2. Cf. Peter Barth, *"Fünfundzwanzig Jahre Calvinforschung, 1909–1934"*; T. H. L. Parker, "A Bibliography and Survey of the British Study of Calvin, 1900–1940"; John T. McNeill, "Thirty Years of Calvin Study"; Hans Rückert, *"Calvin-Literatur seit 1945"*; Joseph N. Tylenda, "Calvin Bibliog-

newed interest in the Reformer's writings. T. H. L. Parker claimed that Barth "showed in a most decisive fashion that the message of the Reformers was valid, *in a new form*, for our own day."[3] This "revolution in Calvin studies,"[4] say some scholars, may yet demonstrate that Calvin was not a Calvinist in the traditional sense at all,[5] that many have actually misunderstood his teaching.

The problem of correctly understanding the voluminous writings of Calvin is not really new, however. One need think only of the question of whether there is a "central doctrine" in Calvin's theology. The variety of answers given and of doctrines proposed illustrates the difficulty. But no matter what doctrine the researcher finally settles on, the doctrine of predestination usually demands attention. Recently the idea of a central doctrine in Calvin's thought has rightly been rejected, and increasing attention has been given to Scripture as the source of Calvin's teachings.[6]

Although there is an abundance of literature on Calvin's thought, it is regrettable that no full-length study of his doctrine of predestination has recently appeared in English.[7] In the light of re-

---

raphy 1960–1970"; Peter De Klerk, "Calvin Bibliography" (1972–   );
Edward A. Dowey, Jr., "Continental Reformation: Works of General Interest: Studies in Calvin and Calvinism Since 1948."

3. "The British Study of Calvin," pp. 127f. Italics added.

4. ". . . the idea of theology being determined by its object, which we owe to Karl Barth, has produced a revolution in Calvin studies as elsewhere." Wilhelm Niesel, *The Theology of Calvin*, p. 17. "The revolution in the approach to the theology of Calvin is unmistakable." Ibid., p. 20.

5. Cf. Parker, "The British Study of Calvin," p. 130; and T. F. Torrance, *Calvin's Doctrine of Man*, pp. 7f.

6. Cf. Otto Weber: "*Calvin hat in seiner 'Institutio' die bedeutendste Dogmatik seiner Zeit geschaffen. Aber diese ist zugleich das, was wir 'Biblische Theologie' nennen. . . . Ein 'Prinzip' seiner Theologie . . . besteht nicht.*" "Calvin," p. 1594. It should be added that many, unfortunately, take this "Biblical" character of Calvin's theology in a Barthian way. For a survey of the various answers to the question of a central doctrine in Calvin, see Paul Jacobs, *Prädestination und Verantwortlichkeit bei Calvin*; Wilhelm Niesel, *The Theology of Calvin*; and Andries D. R. Polman, *De praedestinatieleer van Augustinus, Thomas van Aquino en Calvijn: Een dogmahistorische studie.*

7. This judgment expressed in the first edition of this book in 1961 remains true in 1977 even though many articles and several dissertations have subsequently appeared. Cf. De Klerk, "Calvin Bibliography."

newed interest in Calvin, it is not out of place to attempt a brief presentation of Calvin's doctrine of predestination. Although the question of the centrality of predestination in Calvin's theology continues to draw attention, interest today centers more on such questions as the christocentric character of predestination, the decretive character of reprobation, and the so-called equal ultimacy of election and reprobation. Underlying all of this, there remains of course the vital question of what Calvin's own teaching actually was. Because this survey is concerned primarily with setting forth Calvin's thought on predestination, references to secondary sources and contemporary writers are limited to the footnotes. This is simply an attempt to present Calvin's doctrine of predestination as explained in the *Institutes* and as elaborated and illustrated in his tracts and commentaries.[8] Certain general features of Calvin's doctrine must first be noted; then attention will be directed to election and reprobation, respectively.

The Place of Predestination in the Institutes

Calvin did not invent the doctrine of predestination, nor was he the first to teach it clearly. Calvin's name has become inseparably linked to this doctrine, however, probably because he, more than anyone else, was called upon to defend predestination against all

---

8. The organized discussion of doctrine in the *Institutes* should be given a predominant and guiding role in the exposition of Calvin's views. His attempted brevity in the commentaries was based on the fact that he wished them read in connection with the *Institutes*. (See his letter to the reader in the 1559 Latin edition and his introduction, "Subject Matter of the Present Work," to the 1560 French edition.) Failure to do this ignores Calvin's expressed desire as well as the genetic development of the *Institutes*. Recent studies of Calvin have sometimes shown an undue preference for quoting the commentaries to support new or novel interpretations of his thought. Preference for the theology of the commentaries is openly acknowledged in the preface to *Commentaries*, volume 23 of the Library of Christian Classics. Calvin expressed his disgust at being quoted out of context or in "detached and garbled form" in his letter to the syndics of Geneva, 6 October 1552. *Letters*, 2:349 (OC, 14:379).

sorts of opposition.[9] But the claim that predestination was the central doctrine in Calvin's theology, an a priori principle from which he drew out his whole theological system by logical deduction, is without warrant. He did not engage in speculative, frigid, theoretical reasoning in discussing predestination.

Predestination was certainly not the topic with which Calvin began the *Institutes*. In the final edition of 1559 he did not discuss this subject fully until the end of book 3—about three-fourths of the way into the work. Although he did not arrange his material in the same order in every edition of the *Institutes*,[10] and did not follow the same pattern of arrangement in his various writings on the subject,[11] Calvin never placed predestination at the head of his theology. Unwarranted conclusions are sometimes drawn, however, from the systematic arrangement of the *Institutes*. It is nevertheless worth observing that when later Reformed theologians have discussed predestination along with the decree of God and before discussing creation, they have not followed Calvin's final arrangement of materials.[12]

---

9. In his biography of Calvin, Beza referred to the struggles that had called forth such tracts as *Concerning the Eternal Predestination of God* (1552) and added: "All that Satan gained by these dissensions, was that this article of the Christian religion, which was formerly most obscure, became clear and transparent to all who were not disposed to be contentious." *Tracts and Treatises,* 1:xcvi.

10. In the first edition (1536) predestination is found in the exposition of the article on the church in the Apostles' Creed. In the editions of 1539–1554 the doctrine is treated in the context of soteriology. In the definitive edition of 1559, while this soteriological context is retained, the subject of providence is separated from predestination and brought into book 1. The contention that the relocation of the doctrine of predestination in the various editions of the *Institutes* indicates a growing christocentric interest on Calvin's part is not supported by the evidence. While Calvin is indeed christocentric—christologically theocentric is more accurate—his christocentrism is certainly not that of neo-orthodoxy. Cf. Jacobs, *Prädestination,* p. 71.

11. In the *First Genevan Catechism* (*Instruction in Faith*) of 1537, predestination immediately follows Christology. The *Revised Geneva Catechism* (1542) returned to the arrangement of the *Institutes* of 1536. The *French Confession* (1559) has predestination follow the doctrine of sin and thus precede both Christology and soteriology.

12. Here I am referring only to the arrangement of the material. In doctrinal content, however, I am convinced that there is essential agreement

We find Calvin's treatment of predestination near the end of book 3 in the midst of his discussion of soteriology. A long chapter on prayer[13] precedes the three chapters on predestination, and a chapter on the final resurrection follows it. This contextual factor alone deserves more attention from those who would make predestination the logical core of Calvin's theology. One must also avoid the more common danger today, however, of allowing the systematic place that is given the doctrine to becloud the very things Calvin says clearly in this section, and the fundamental importance that the doctrine has within the whole of his thought.[14] While predestination is not Calvin's central doctrine, it is nonetheless of crucial importance for his entire, Biblically derived theology.[15]

This systematic or methodological placement of the doctrine of predestination in the *Institutes*, then, makes the immediate context of Calvin's discussion important. Soteriology concerns the Holy Spirit's work in applying to sinners the completed atoning work of Christ. In this work the Holy Spirit employs men as His agents in the preaching of the gospel. The gospel is not preached to all, however, and where it is preached, it meets with different responses. How is this to be explained? This question provides the context of Calvin's discussion of predestination, as is clear from his opening words:

---

between classic Reformed theologians, such as Herman Bavinck, and Calvin. This is not to deny the introduction of some elements in the seventeenth century and carried on by later theologians that differ significantly from Calvin. The Canons of Dort (1618–1619) are also in essential agreement with the theology of Calvin.

13. The passage on prayer (3.20) is by itself slightly longer than Calvin's entire discussion of predestination (3.21–24).

14. In this connection Karl Barth interestingly found it necessary to chide Niesel for minimizing the central importance of predestination in Calvin's thought. Barth saw predestination "in some degree the consummation of the doctrine of reconciliation . . . the ultimate and decisive word which sheds additional light on all that has gone before." *Church Dogmatics*, 2 (part 2): 85; *Die kirchliche Dogmatik*, 2 (part 2): 92.

15. Polman is correct in seeing it as a doctrine that is *"in geloofsgehoorzaamheid aan Gods Woord, uit de Schriftgegevens opgebouwd. Dat er achteraf verband met de andere leerstukken bestaat, komt bij hem alleen voort uit het feit, dat God zelf zich in Zijn openbaring niet weerspreekt."* De praedestinatieleer, pp. 309f.

In actual fact, the covenant of life is not preached equally among all men, and among those to whom it is preached, it does not gain the same acceptance either constantly or in equal degree. In this diversity the wonderful depth of God's judgment is made known. For there is no doubt that this variety also serves the decision of God's eternal election. If it is plain that it comes to pass by God's bidding that salvation is freely offered to some while others are barred from access to it, at once great and difficult questions spring up, explicable only when reverent minds regard as settled what they may suitably hold concerning election and predestination.[16]

Such was also the context of Paul's significant discussion of pre-destination in Romans 9, a chapter especially decisive in Calvin's various discussions of the doctrine.[17] There can be no doubt that Calvin's careful study of the Epistle to the Romans, his commentary on which was published in 1539, was the source of the doctrine of predestination and also the major influence on his rearrangement of the materials in the second edition of the *Institutes* in 1539.[18]

We shall return to this matter of the soteriological context of Calvin's discussion of predestination when we deal specifically with

---

16. 3.21.1 (OS, 4:368). ". . . *nec enim dubium quin aeternae Dei electionis arbitrio haec quoque varietas serviat.*" (Here and below the quotations from the Latin will usually include only the most relevant words rather than the entire quotation.) Here as in other places Calvin used the term *election* as equivalent to *predestination.* Note the title he gave to 3.21: "*De electione aeterna, qua Deus alios ad salutem, alios ad interitum praedestinavit.*" The English translation of the *Institutes* used here and throughout this book is that of Ford Lewis Battles.

17. Cf. Calvin's summary of the argument of Romans 9 in *The Epistles of Paul the Apostle to the Romans and to the Thessalonians,* p. 9 (OC, 49:1–6), and comments on Romans 9:1–5 (OC, 49:7–12). For lengthy discussions of Romans 9, see in addition *Institutes* 3.22.4–6, 11; and *Eternal Predestination,* pp. 76ff.

18. Cf. Bavinck, *Gereformeerde dogmatiek,* 2:319. Polman said: "*In zijn verklaring van den brief aan de Romeinen heeft Calvijn, in volstrekte geloofsgehoorzaamheid aan de Schriftopenbaring zijn praedestinatieleer vastgesteld. Al wat later volgt, is niet dan breedere uitwerking, zonder dat een bepaalde ontwikkeling kan geconstateerd.*" (Polman italicized this concluding sentence of his work.) *De praedestinatieleer,* p. 355. See also Jacobs, *Prädestination,* pp. 61ff.

election and reprobation. But it is important to observe this context at the outset of this study.

The Practical Significance of Predestination

Within a soteriological context one would hardly expect to find a frigid, speculative discussion of the eternal predestination of God. One of the ironies of history is that the man who wrote that "no one can be more averse to paradox than I am, and in subtleties I find no delight at all,"[19] should repeatedly be accused of being and doing just that.[20] A sympathetic reading of the *Institutes* should quickly dispel the myth.

The opening words of the 1559 *Institutes* indicate that its author had made a clear break with the scholastics. Calvin spoke not of *scientia* but of *sapientia*, "wisdom."[21] His definition of the knowledge of God shows his practical religious concern: "Now, the knowledge of God, as I understand it, is that by which we not only conceive that there is a God but also grasp what befits us and is proper to his glory, in fine, what is to our advantage to know of him. Indeed, we shall not say that, properly speaking, God is known where there is no religion or piety."[22] When Calvin considered the providence of God, he said that it is "expedient here to discuss briefly to what end Scripture teaches that all things are divinely ordained." By means of "pious and holy meditation on providence, which the rule of piety dictates to us," Calvin wished to receive "the best and

---

19. "*Ego certe, si quis alius, semper a paradoxis abhorri et argutiis minime dilector.*" To Laelius Socinus in 1551. *Letters*, 2:315 (OC, 14:230).

20. "*Freilich hat Calvin sich seit 1539 trotz standiger Warnung vor der Spekulation dennoch auf deren Bahn drangen lassen, indem er zwischen Erwahlung und Verwerfung logisch eine Alternative aufrichtete und damit zum Gedanken der gemina praedestinatio kam, der vorweg geschehen (auch vor dem Sundenfall liegenden, 'supralapsarischen') Bestimmung, die electio oder reprobatio bedeutete.*" Weber, "Calvin," p. 1594. Torrance thought that Calvin had not avoided "arid, logical forms," making "distinctions too clean and too rigid," in the doctrines of predestination and providence, but that he had attained high success with other doctrines. *Calvin's Doctrine of Man*, pp. 7f.

21. 1.1.1 (OS, 3:31). "*Tota fere sapientiae nostrae summa. . . .*"

22. Ibid., 1.2.1 (OS, 3:34). "*Dei notitiam. . . .*"

sweetest fruit."[23] Throughout the *Institutes* this practical concern pervades Calvin's discussion of election and reprobation. The preacher-pastor-theologian always demonstrated a warm, practical interest in the doctrines that he learned from Scripture.

Calvin acknowledged that the consideration of this doctrine immediately presents very difficult questions. He considered these questions inexplicable if the Biblical view of predestination is not maintained. But Calvin did not begin with these problems. He first called attention to the "usefulness of this doctrine" and to "its very sweet fruit."[24] He mentioned three of these fruits: this doctrine teaches us to put our trust in the free mercy of God; it exalts the glory of God; and it fosters sincere humility.

Contemplation of divine predestination teaches us to look at the mercy of God. In Calvin's judgment "we shall never be clearly persuaded, as we ought to be, that our salvation flows from the wellspring of God's free mercy until we come to know his eternal election, which illumines God's grace by this contrast: that he does not indiscriminately adopt all into the hope of salvation but gives to some what he denies to others."[25] Salvation does not come from our works; election makes clear "that our salvation comes about solely from God's mere generosity."[26] Those who "shut the gates" to this doctrine "wrong men no less than God"; nothing will "suffice to make us humble as we ought to be nor shall we otherwise sincerely feel how much we are obliged to God" unless we contemplate His election. Hence "ignorance of this principle detracts from God's glory" and "takes away from true humility."[27]

Those who are blind to the three benefits of this doctrine—God's free mercy, God's glory, our sincere humility—"would wish the foundation of our salvation to be removed from our midst" and would "very badly serve the interests of themselves and of all other

---

23. Ibid., 1.17.6 (OS, 3:209).

24. Ibid., 3.21.1 (OS, 4:369). ". . . *non modo utilitas huius doctrinae, sed suavissimus quoque fructus se profert.*"

25. Ibid.

26. Ibid. "*Electioni gratuitae . . . ex mera Dei liberalitate . . . ad electionis originem.*"

27. Ibid.

believers."[28] In this doctrine one discovers the very origin of Christ's church. The comfort of God's predestination is not for individuals alone; it is for the church and the communion of believers. We hear Calvin preach: "Let us resort to the election of God, whenever we become dismayed or cast down: if we see men fall away, if the whole church should seem to come to nought, we must remember that God hath his foundation; that is, the church is not grounded upon the will of man, for they did not make themselves, neither can they reform themselves: but this proceedeth from the pure goodness and mercy of God."[29]

This useful doctrine with its pleasant fruits "ought to be preached openly and fully."[30] "They that think to abolish the doctrine of God's election destroy as much as possible the salvation of the world."[31] In fact "the devil hath no fitter instrument than those who fight against predestination; and cannot in their rage suffer it to be spoken of, or preached as it ought to be."[32] "The devil can find no better means to destroy our faith, than to hide this article from our view."[33]

This nonspeculative, deeply religious and practical interest is evident also in what is regarded as one of Calvin's most polemic tracts, *Concerning the Eternal Predestination of God* (1552). In his response to the charges of Albert Pighius, archdeacon of Utrecht, Calvin stated that he really had nothing more to say than he had

---

28. Ibid. (OS, 4:370).

29. On II Tim. 2:19. *Sermons on the Epistles of S. Paule to Timothie and Titus,* p. 823a (OC, 54:170f.). Calvin added: "As the election of God is to give us a sure constancy, to make us happy in the midst of trouble, which otherwise might disquiet us, we must not cease to call on him. . . ." Ibid., p. 824a (OC, 54:171f.).

30. On II Tim. 1:8–9. Ibid., p. 706a (OC, 54:51). Calvin also warned against improper preaching and praying with respect to predestination in the *Institutes,* 3.23.14; 3.24.5.

31. Ibid., p. 704a (OC, 54:49).

32. Ibid., p. 704b. "There is more honesty in the papists than in these men," said Calvin, preaching on II Timothy 1:9–10; hence these men ought to be detested even more than the papists. Ibid., p. 707b (OC, 54:53).

33. On II Tim. 2:19. Ibid., p. 823b (OC, 54:171).

stated in the *Institutes*, but then he provided this remarkable summary of his practical concern:

> The *Institutes* testify fully and abundantly to what I think, even should I add nothing besides. First of all, I beg my readers to recall the admonition made there. This matter is not a subtle and obscure speculation, as they falsely think, which wearies the mind without profit. It is rather a solid argument excellently fitted to the use of the godly. For it builds up faith soundly, trains us to humility, elevates us to admiration of the immense goodness of God towards us, and excites us to praise this goodness. There is no consideration more apt for the building up of faith than that we should listen to this election which the Spirit of God testifies in our hearts to stand in the eternal and inflexible goodwill of God, invulnerable to all storms of the world, all assaults of Satan and all vacillation of the flesh. For then indeed our salvation is assured to us, since we find its cause in the breast of God. For thus we lay hold of life in Christ made manifest to faith, so that, led by the same faith, we can penetrate farther to see from what source this life proceeds. Confidence of salvation is founded upon Christ and rests on the promises of the gospel. Nor is it a negligible support when, believing in Christ, we hear that this is divinely given to us, that before the beginning of the world we were both ordained to faith and also elected to the inheritance of heavenly life. Hence arises an impregnable security.[34]

The Biblical Source of Predestination

The theologian's task, according to Calvin, "is not to divert the ears with chatter, but to strengthen consciences by teaching things true, sure, and profitable."[35] Nor is the theologian himself to determine what is true, sure, and profitable; that is given by Scripture alone. "For our wisdom ought to be nothing else than to embrace

---

34. *Eternal Predestination*, pp. 56f. (OC, 8:260).
35. *Institutes* 1.14.4 (OS, 3:157).

with humble teachableness, and at least without finding fault, whatever is taught in Sacred Scripture."[36] "We ought to seek from Scripture a sure rule for both thinking and speaking to which both the thoughts of our minds and the words of our mouths should be conformed."[37] For Calvin, Scripture is the inspired and inerrant Word of God.[38] As the revealed will of the living God, Scripture is the single source of Calvin's theology.

Why is Calvin so concerned to explain and defend the doctrine of predestination? He stated: "I can declare with all truth that I should never have spoken on this subject, unless the Word of God had led the way, as indeed all godly readers of my earlier writings, and especially of my *Institutes*, will readily gather."[39] After defining predestination in the light of his Scriptural study, he advised his readers "not to take a prejudiced position on either side until, when the passages of Scripture have been adduced, it shall be clear what opinion ought to be held."[40] He drew the doctrine from Scripture; that is also the standard by which he wanted his exposition judged. It is not speculatively produced with isolated proof texts attached. Many passages are quoted, but the basic structure of the doctrine is dependent on Scripture, especially on Romans and Ephesians. Calvin's first commentary was on Romans, and his study of that book greatly influenced his elaboration of the doctrine of predestination in the *Institutes*.[41] Calvin was convinced that "if we understand this

---

36. Ibid., 1.18.4 (OS, 3:227). But for one sentence, this is the conclusion of book 1.

37. Ibid., 1.13.3 (OS, 3:112). This statement underwent frequent careful revisions during the various editions.

38. See ibid., 1.6–9. Although this has also become a disputed issue, I believe the following studies have provided ample evidence for the statement: Edward A. Dowey, Jr., *The Knowledge of God in Calvin's Theology*, pp. 90ff.; Kenneth S. Kantzer, "Calvin and the Holy Scriptures"; and John Murray, *Calvin on Scripture and Divine Sovereignty*, pp. 11–51.

39. *Eternal Predestination*, pp. 61f. (OC, 8:265).

40. *Institutes* 3.21.7 (OS, 4:378).

41. See notes 10 and 18 above. Amazingly different, and failing to give due account to Calvin's study of Romans, is Peter Barth's conjecture that Calvin's miserable experiences with the citizens of Geneva led him to the development of double predestination in the edition of 1539: "*Sollten am Ende die bösen Erfahrungen, die der junge Calvin mit den Einwohnern*

Epistle, we have a passage opened to us to the understanding of the whole of Scripture."[42]

An axiom for Calvin is that the theologian must be obedient to the teaching of God's Word: "We ought to have such respect for the Word of God that any difference of interpretation on our part should alter it as little as possible. . . . It is therefore presumptuous and almost blasphemous to turn the meaning of Scripture around without due care, as though it were some game that we were playing."[43] When accused by his opponents of originating the doctrine that relates the hardening of men to the eternal counsel of God, Calvin emphatically replied: "We are certainly not the author of this opinion. . . . Paul taught this before us. . . . For in the present matter we contend for nothing which is not taught by him."[44] To those who stumble at Paul's distinction between election and reprobation in Romans 9, Calvin responded, "But what audacity to check the Holy Spirit and Paul!"[45]

While insisting that Scripture must be the exclusive source[46] of this doctrine, Calvin recognized especially two dangers that arise in dealing with Scripture. It is possible, on the one hand, to engage in excessive curiosity that leads to speculation beyond what Scripture teaches. On the other hand, it is possible to fall prey to an excessive timidity that dares not speak where the Scriptures do speak. With respect to the first, he wrote: "Human curiosity ren-

---

Genfs hatte machen müssen über Gebühr mitgeredet haben, als er als Vertriebener in Basel die zweite Institutio ausarbeitete?" "Die biblische Grundlage der Prädestinationslehre bei Calvin," in *De l'election eternelle de Dieu,* p. 44.

42. Preface to *Romans,* p. 3. See also *Commentaries,* pp. 73f.

43. Ibid., *Romans,* pp. 3f.

44. *Eternal Predestination,* p. 60 (OC, 8:263).

45. *Romans* (on 9:14). OC, 49:181.

46. Karl Barth thought Calvin gave too much attention to a second source, "experience" or "would-be experience." *Church Dogmatics,* 2 (part 2): 39–41; *Die kirchliche Dogmatik,* 2 (part 2): 40–43. While it is true that Calvin often spoke of "experience," the expression is accurately explained in the following: *"Hij . . . blijft geheel uit de Schrift, die de ervaring van elken dag verklaart en bevestigt, spreken."* Polman, *De Praedestinatieleer,* p. 343. *"Steeds klimt hij vanuit de aardsche werkelijkheid, die uit de Schrift belicht wordt, tot Gods decreet op."* Ibid., p. 349.

ders the discussion of predestination, already somewhat difficult of itself, very confusing and even dangerous. No restraints can hold it back from wandering in forbidden bypaths and thrusting upward to the heights. If allowed, it will leave no secret to God that it will not search out and unravel."[47] Those who are tempted by this danger of speculation must remember that when they inquire into predestination, "they are penetrating the sacred precincts of divine wisdom. If anyone with carefree assurance breaks into this place, he will not succeed in satisfying his curiosity and he will enter a labyrinth from which he can find no exit. For it is not right for man unrestrainedly to search out things that the Lord has willed to be hid in himself, and to unfold from eternity itself the sublimest wisdom, which he would have us revere but not understand that through this also he should fill us with wonder."[48] What God reveals in Scripture of the secrets of His will, "these he decided to reveal in so far as he foresaw that they would concern us and benefit us."[49] But "the moment we exceed the bounds of the Word, our course is outside the pathway and in darkness, and . . . there we must repeatedly wander, slip, and stumble."[50] Against this danger Calvin warned: "Let this, therefore, first of all be before our eyes: to seek any other knowledge of predestination than what the Word of God discloses is not less insane than if one should purpose to walk in a pathless waste [cf. Job 12:24], or to see in darkness. And let us not be ashamed to be ignorant of something in this matter, wherein there is a certain learned ignorance."[51]

Calvin also issued warnings against the opposite danger of those "who are so cautious or fearful that they desire to bury predestination in order not to disturb weak souls."[52] The Christian must "open his mind and ears to every utterance of God directed to him," but "when the Lord closes his holy lips, he also shall at once close the way to inquiry."[53] This is Calvin's concern:

---

47. *Institutes* 3.21.1 (OS, 4:370).
48. Ibid.
49. Ibid.
50. Ibid., 3.21.2 (OS, 4:371).
51. Ibid.
52. Ibid., 3.21.4 (OS, 4:373).
53. Ibid., 3.21.3 (OS, 4:372).

> For Scripture is the school of the Holy Spirit, in which, as
> nothing is omitted that is both necessary and useful to know,
> so nothing is taught but what is expedient to know. Therefore
> we must guard against depriving believers of anything dis-
> closed about predestination in Scripture, lest we seem either
> wickedly to defraud them of the blessing of their God or to
> accuse and scoff at the Holy Spirit for having published what
> it is in any way profitable to suppress. . . . The best limit
> of sobriety for us will be not only to follow God's lead always
> in learning but, when he sets an end to teaching, to stop
> trying to be wise.[54]

Profane men carp, rail, bark, or scoff at predestination, but if opposition to Scriptural doctrine were to deter the Christian, he would
be required to keep secret also the doctrines of the Trinity and
creation, in fact, all "the chief doctrines of the faith."[55]

The Biblical source of all doctrine and the dangers to be avoided
are expressed in this general rule: "I desire only to have them generally admit that we should not investigate what the Lord has left
hidden in secret, that we should not neglect what he has brought
into the open, so that we may not be convicted of excessive curiosity on the one hand, or of excessive ingratitude on the other."[56]
Calvin's desire was that there might flourish in the church of God
"sufficient greatness of soul" to "prevent its godly teachers from
being ashamed of the simple profession of true doctrine, however
hated it may be," and "to refute whatever reproaches the ungodly
may pour forth."[57]

The Definition of Predestination

Calvin taught the doctrine of predestination because he was convinced that this is what Scripture demands. He attempted to avoid

---

54. Ibid. See *Romans* (on 9:14) for similar words. OC, 49:180–81. This
similarity is evident at many points.

55. Ibid., 3.21.4 (OS, 4:372).

56. Ibid. (OS, 4:373).

57. *Romans* (on 9:14). OC, 49:181.

speculation and theorizing so that the pleasant fruits of the Scriptural doctrine may be tasted, and he did this in a soteriological context that reflects the powerful influence of the Epistle to the Romans. Before proceeding to sketch Calvin's view of election and reprobation, respectively, it will be useful to survey the entire doctrine before us. His definitions provide good summaries of the whole.

In the two comprehensive definitions that follow, Calvin summarized his doctrine of double predestination:

> We call predestination God's eternal decree, by which he determined with himself what he willed to become of each man. For all are not created in equal condition; rather, eternal life is foreordained for some, eternal damnation for others. Therefore, as any man has been created to one or the other of these ends, we speak of him as predestined to life or death.[58]

> As Scripture, then, clearly shows, we say that God once established by his eternal and unchangeable plan those whom he long before determined once for all to receive into salvation, and those whom, on the other hand, he would devote to destruction. We assert that, with respect to the elect, this plan was founded upon his freely given mercy, without regard to human worth; but by his just and irreprehensible but incomprehensible judgment he has barred the door of life to those whom he has given over to damnation. Now among the elect we regard the call as a testimony of election. Then we hold justification another sign of its manifestation, until they come into the glory in which the fulfillment of that election lies. But as the Lord seals his elect by call and justification, so, by shutting off the reprobate from knowledge of his name or from the sanctification of his Spirit, he, as it were, reveals by these marks what sort of judgment awaits them.[59]

58. Ibid., 3.21.5 (OS, 4:374). *"Praedestinationem vocamus aeternum Dei decretum, quo apud se constitutum habuit quid de unoquoque homine fieri vellet. Non enim pari conditione creantur omnes: sed aliis vita aeterna, aliis damnatio aeterna praeordinatur. Itaque prout in alterutrum finem quisque conditus est, ita vel ad vitam vel ad mortem praedestinatum dicimus."*

59. Ibid., 3.21.7 (OS, 4:378f.). *"Quod ergo Scriptura clare ostendit,*

Almost everything that Calvin taught regarding predestination is included in these two summaries.

In other writings Calvin presented similar summaries. In the preface to his commentary on the Psalms, he spoke of "eternal predestination by which God distinguished the reprobate from the elect."[60] In refuting the arguments of Pighius, the first of three considerations cited by Calvin is this: ". . . the eternal predestination of God, by which before the fall of Adam He decreed what should take place concerning the whole human race and every individual, was fixed and determined."[61] Finally, we note Calvin's early summary in *Instruction in Faith* (1537). The focus is similar to that of Romans 9 and of the final edition of the *Institutes*:

> Beyond this contrast of attitudes of believers and unbelievers, the great secret of God's counsel must necessarily be considered. For, the seed of the word of God takes root and brings forth fruit only in those whom the Lord, by his eternal election, has predestined to be children and heirs of the heavenly kingdom. To all the others (who by the same counsel of God are rejected before the foundation of the world) the clear and evident preaching of truth can be nothing but an odor of death unto death. . . . We acknowledge, therefore, the elect to be recipients of his mercy (as truly they are) and the rejected to be recipients of his wrath, a wrath, however, which is nothing but just.[62]

---

dicimus aeterno et immutabili consilio Deum semel constituisse quos olim semel assumere vellet in salutem, quos rursum exitio devovere; hoc consilium quoad electos in gratuita eius misericordia fundatum esse asserimus, nullo humanae dignitatis respectu; quos vero damnationi addicit, his iusto quidem et irreprehensibili, sed incomprehensibili ipsius iudicio, vitae aditum praecludi. Iam vero in electis vocationem statuimus, electionis testimonium. Iustificationem deinde, alterum eius manifestandae symbolum, donec ad gloriam in qua eius complementum extat pervenitur. Quemadmodum autem vocatione et iustificatione electos suos Dominus signat, ita reprobos vel a notitia sui nominis, vel a Spiritus sui sanctificatione excludendo, quale maneat eos iudicium istis veluti notis aperit."

60. *Commentaries*, pp. 51–57 (OC, 31:29).

61. *Eternal Predestination*, p. 121 (OC, 8:313).

62. *Instruction in Faith*, pp. 36f. (OC, 22:46–47). See also the *Articles Concerning Predestination*: ". . . upon the same decree depends the

These summaries make clear that Calvin held to double predestination, that is, to both election and reprobation. These summaries and the whole of his teaching indicate that Calvin considered both election and reprobation sovereign works of God rooted in the eternal and immutable decree or eternal counsel of the Triune God. Thus Calvin emphasized both sovereign election and sovereign reprobation. We shall see, however, that Calvin used other adjectives that cannot be applied to election and reprobation equally. He followed Paul in speaking of both election and reprobation: ". . . in the case of the elect he would have us contemplate the mercy of God, but in the case of the reprobate acknowledge His righteous judgment."[63]

Election is gratuitous election that displays the free mercy and goodness of God. The elect are elect in Christ; Christ is the mirror of election. Reprobation, on the other hand, displays the righteous judgment of God, His justice. That is not to imply that justice does not also characterize God's election; it certainly does, for "there can be no injustice at all either to the elect or the reprobate."[64] In all His works God is perfectly just. Gratuitous mercy, however, does not characterize God's sovereign reprobation. Hence we reflect Calvin's emphasis when we speak of sovereign and gratuitous election on the one hand, and of sovereign and just (righteous) reprobation on the other. Other attributes of God also appear in predestination, of course. The incomprehensibility of God is called to our attention again and again, but the three attributes mentioned —sovereignty, grace, and justice—are the chief ones mentioned in

---

distinction between elect and reprobate: as he adopted some for himself for salvation, he destined others for eternal ruin." In *Theological Treatises*, p. 179 (OC, 9:713). In his *Defence of the Secret Providence of God* (1558) Calvin used the term *predestination* in the sense of "providence": "But *predestination* I define to be, according to the Holy Scriptures, that free and unfettered counsel of God by which He rules all mankind, and all men and things, and also all parts and particles of the world by His infinite wisdom and incomprehensible justice." In *Calvin's Calvinism*, p. 261 (OC, 9:287).

63. *Romans* (on 9:14), p. 203 (OC, 49:180).

64. Ibid.

Calvin's discussion. From this survey of the general features of Calvin's doctrine of predestination, we now turn to a more detailed examination first of sovereign and gratuitous election, and then of sovereign and just reprobation.

Chapter 2

Sovereign and Gratuitous Election

IN SETTING FORTH the Biblical basis for the doctrine of election, Calvin begins in his *Institutes* with Ephesians and then goes to Romans. In that great trinitarian doxology of Ephesians 1, Paul addressed "the saints in Ephesus, the faithful in Christ Jesus" (NIV). He referred to God's "pleasure and will" as the source of all the grace they had received: "Praise be to the God and Father of our Lord Jesus Christ, who has blessed us in the heavenly realms with every spiritual blessing in Christ. For he chose us in him before the creation of the world to be holy and blameless in his sight. In love he predestined us to be adopted as sons through Jesus Christ, in accordance with his pleasure and will—to the praise of his glorious grace, which he has freely given us in the One he loves." (Eph. 1:3–6 NIV)

When one pays attention to the separate clauses of this passage and ties them all together, there is no reason to doubt the doctrine of election. Calvin's comments on this passage give us a summary of the main features of the doctrine of sovereign and gratuitous election:

> Since he calls them "elect," it cannot be doubted that he is speaking to believers, as he also soon declares. . . . By saying that they were "elect before the creation of the world" [Eph. 1:4], he takes away all regard for worth. For what basis for distinction is there among those who did not yet exist, and

29

who were subsequently to be equals in Adam? Now if they are elect in Christ, it follows that not only is each man elected without respect to his own person but also certain ones are separated from others, since we see that not all are members of Christ. Besides, the fact that they were elected "to be holy" [Eph. 1:4b] plainly refutes the error that derives election from foreknowledge, since Paul declares all virtue appearing in man is the result of election. Now if a higher cause be sought, Paul answers that God has predestined it so, and that this is "according to the good pleasure of his will" [Eph. 1:5b]. By these words he does away with all means of their election that men imagine in themselves. For all benefits that God bestows for the spiritual life, as Paul teaches, flow from this one source: namely, that God has chosen whom he has willed, and before their birth has laid up for them individually the grace that he willed to grant them.[1]

In his commentary on Ephesians Calvin summarized the doctrine of election by referring to four causes of our salvation: "The efficient cause is the good pleasure of the will of God; the material cause is Christ; and the final cause is the praise of His grace. . . . The formal cause [is] the preaching of the Gospel, by which the goodness of God flows out to us."[2] Although Calvin did not employ these Aristotelian terms in the *Institutes*, he did make the same distinctions throughout his discussion of election. We shall consider the various elements of Calvin's discussion under the following divisions: the divine decree, its cause and ground, its goal and means.

The Divine Decree of Election

In this section we shall survey Calvin's emphasis upon three fac-

---

1. 3.22.2 (OS, 4:381f.). See also *Concerning the Eternal Predestination of God*, pp. 68, 126, 128, 134, 140, 145, 158.

2. *The Epistles of Paul the Apostle to the Galatians, Ephesians, Philippians and Colossians* (on Eph. 1:5, 8). OC, 51:148, 150. (This commentary was first published in 1548; the section of the *Institutes* quoted above first appeared in the 1559 edition.) T. F. Torrance said that Calvin had viewed Christ as the cause of election in all four senses. *Kingdom and Church*, pp. 73, 107. I consider this a neo-orthodox reading of Calvin.

tors: election is *God's* work; election is God's *decretive* work; and, finally, election is God's decretive work relating to *individuals*.

Election is God's work. According to Calvin, election is from beginning to end the sovereign work of our gracious God. Election as God's work concerns the eternal counsel made before the foundation of the world. As God's work, election concerns the salvation of men and women that is wrought entirely by our sovereign God. The final end of election is not attained until God, having worked the salvation of His elect and having brought them to glory, is thereby fully glorified Himself.

Although this divine decree is in some sense the work of all three persons of the Trinity, Calvin understood it as primarily the work of the first two persons. That the Father is the author of the decree is most clear. It is in the light of the Father's eternal decree that Christ's words must be understood: "All that the Father gives me will come to me. . . . And this is the will of him who sent me, that I shall lose none of all that he has given me. . . ."[3] Thus "the Father's gift is the beginning of our reception into the surety and protection of Christ."[4]

But Calvin also considered Christ Himself author of the decree of election: "Meanwhile, although Christ interposes himself as mediator, he claims for himself, in common with the Father, the right to choose."[5] This is the meaning of Jesus' words in John 13:18: "I am not referring to all of you; I know those I have chosen" (NIV). Thus when Christ declared "that he knows whom he has chosen, he denotes in the human genus a particular species, distinguished not by the quality of its virtues but by heavenly decree. . . . Christ makes himself the Author of election."[6] Shortly we shall also see that Calvin regarded the elect as "elect in Christ" and that he viewed Christ as "the mirror of our election." But it is important here to see that Christ is Himself author of the decree.

---

3. John 6:37, 39 (NIV) in 3.22.7.

4. *Institutes* 3.22.7 (OS, 4:387).

5. Ibid.

6. Ibid. ". . . *caeleste decreto . . . quando se Christus electionis facit authorem. . . .*" Cf. comments on John 13:18 in *The Gospel According to St. John and the First Epistle of John* (OC, 47:310–11).

We have noticed that Calvin regarded the divine decree as the work of all three persons of the Trinity,[7] but that he emphasized the roles of the Father and the Son. He did not explicitly refer to the Holy Spirit as author of the decree as he did the Father and the Son. The Holy Spirit is involved in the doctrine of election, of course: He is the teacher of this doctrine, having inspired the Scriptures,[8] and even more significantly, His soteriological work carries out the eternal decree of God.[9]

Election is God's decretive work. God's works are many and varied. The decretive work of God is here in focus. To understand Calvin, one must recognize that election, as well as reprobation, refers to the sovereign, eternal counsel of God. "We call predestination *God's eternal decree*, by which he determined with himself what he willed to become of each man."[10] "Scripture . . . clearly shows . . . that God once established *by his eternal and unchangeable plan* those whom he long before determined once for all to receive unto salvation, and those whom, on the other hand, he would devote to destruction."[11] Calvin spoke of the eternal decree, or the eternal counsel or plan: it precedes the existence of the person elected (e.g., Jacob); it precedes the fall of Adam;[12] indeed, it precedes the creation of the world.[13] That is why Calvin said that "all are not created in equal condition; rather, eternal life is foreordained for some, eternal damnation for others."[14] Calvin was not

---

7. See *Institutes* 1.13 and 1.16–18 (OS, 3:108ff., 187ff.).

8. See ibid., 1.6–9 (OS, 3:60ff.).

9. The whole of book 3, "*De modo percipiendae Christi gratiae*"; and 3.1, "*Quae de Christo dicta sunt, nobis prodesse, arcana operatione Spiritus.*" OS, 4:1.

10. *Institutes* 3.21.5 (OS, 4:374). Italics added. See chap. 1, note 58 above.

11. Ibid., 3.21.7 (OS, 4:378f.). Italics added. See chap. 1, note 59 above.

12. *Eternal Predestination*, p. 121 (OC, 8:313).

13. *Ephesians* (on 1:4). OC, 51:147. It is important to observe that, although the relation of time and eternity is a complex question, Calvin did not use the word *precede* in a figurative sense as Edward A. Dowey, Jr., seems to have done. *The Knowledge of God in Calvin's Theology*, p. 187.

14. *Institutes* 3.21.5 (OS, 4:374). See chap. 1, note 58 above.

speculating about the order of the decrees.[15] Rather, with complete Biblical warrant he was speaking of the eternal counsel of God that precedes all His activities in history, an eternal counsel that is, however, carried out in history.

Calvin's reference to the eternal counsel and decree of God indicates the intimate relationship between predestination and providence in his thought. In the editions of the *Institutes* published from 1539 to 1554, Calvin discussed these subjects together in the same chapter. Not until the final edition of 1559 did he move his discussion of predestination to book 3. This systematic rearrangement did not, however, involve a change in content nor a basic change in Calvin's thought. When he discussed providence, he found it necessary to refer to predestination—to election and reprobation. And when he here discussed predestination, the whole is related to the counsel of God that is executed through His providential direction and government of all things.

In the light of contemporary discussion, this point deserves further attention. Reference to God's decree of election at once recalls Calvin's assertions in connection with God's providence: "But we make God the ruler and governor of all things, who in accordance with his wisdom has from the farthest limit of eternity decreed what he was going to do, and now by his might carries out what he has decreed."[16] He called us to "remember that there is no erratic power, or action, or motion in creatures, but that they are governed by God's secret plan in such a way that nothing happens

---

15. It is unwarranted, without further distinctions, to claim that Calvin was supralapsarian. See Otto Weber, "Calvin," p. 1594; Dowey, *The Knowledge of God*, p. 186; Wilhelm-Albert Hauck, *Die Erwählten: Prädestination und Heilsgewissheit nach Calvin*, p. 19; *De l'election eternelle de Dieu: Actes du congres international de theologie calviniste, Geneve, 15–18 Juin 1936*. While Calvin may be called a supralapsarian in the earlier usage of that term, later both infralapsarians and supralapsarians agreed that Adam's fall had been decreed by God. Calvin did not speculate about a logical order of the divine decrees and hence is not a supralapsarian in the later sense of the term. See Andries D. R. Polman, *De praedestinatieleer van Augustinus, Thomas van Aquino en Calvijn: Een dogmahistorische studie*, pp. 348f., 377; Heinz Otten, *Calvins theologische Anschauung von der Prädestination*, pp. 97f.

16. *Institutes* 1.16.8 (OS, 3:198f.).

except what is knowingly and willingly decreed by him."[17] In this summary of the whole doctrine of providence, he made direct mention of election and reprobation: "To sum up, since God's will is said to be the cause of all things, I have made his providence the determinative principle for all human plans and works, not only in order to display its force in the elect, who are ruled by the Holy Spirit, but also to compel the reprobate to obedience."[18]

Election is particular. According to Calvin the decretive work of God is specific and particular; it concerns specific individuals. The decree of election does not concern only some general intention of God, nor is it a decree only to save those who believe. Rather, the decree concerns individuals (not yet existing, of course) whom God destines for eternal salvation; this decree provides the means for accomplishing that purpose for each elect individual. Calvin's view of individual election did not, however, lead him to individualism.

Calvin did not refer exclusively to individual election, and it is important to notice this in order to understand the sections on predestination properly. He speaks of a national election of Israel and of an election to office in distinction from individual election to salvation. These other "species" or "degrees"[19] of election display

---

17. Ibid., 1.16.3 (OS, 3:192). Cf. 3.23.6: ". . . the disposition of all things is in God's hand. . . . it is clear that all things take place rather by his determination and bidding."

18. Ibid., 1.18.2 (OS, 3:223). Cf. also 3.24.17, where reference is obviously made to 1.18. Note also 3.23.3, 5, 6 (frequently), 8, 9, where the words *predestination* and *providence* are used, sometimes interchangeably. Although Torrance is correct in saying that Calvin did not view election as *pars providentiae* in the sense that Aquinas did, Torrance did not do justice to the intimate relation of these doctrines in Calvin. *Kingdom and Church*, p. 4. Cf. Hauck, *Vorsehung und Freiheit nach Calvin*, pp. 11ff., 20f.; Hauck, *Die Erwählten*, pp. 33ff.; and Paul Jacobs, *Prädestination und Verantwortlichkeit bei Calvin*, pp. 67f.

19. *Institutes* 3.21.6 (OS, 4:376–77). The Latin has *"secundus gradus"* and *"duos gradus."* See also on John 13:18 (OC, 47:310–11). Dowey did not accurately reproduce Calvin in this section: "The whole tortuous teaching about the 'degrees' of election is simply Calvin trying to extricate his doctrine from the implications of his own inerrancy view of Scripture. On the basis of mere formal Biblicism, Calvin realizes that he would have

the generosity as well as the sovereignty of God's election; they do not necessarily involve salvation, however. Esau, for example, was a member of the elect nation, but he broke the covenant and showed that he was not elect to salvation. The same was true of Ishmael. Judas is one who was both a member of the elect nation and was elected to office, but who was not elected to salvation. "Although it is now sufficiently clear that God by his secret plan freely chooses whom he pleases, rejecting others," Calvin continued, "still his free election has been only half explained until we come to *individual persons*, to whom God not only offers salvation but so assigns it that the certainty of its effect is not in suspense or doubt."[20] Not the whole nation of Israel but only those individually elected unto salvation are "engrafted to their Head," Jesus Christ, so "they are never cut off from salvation."[21] These elect persons are, however, bound together into a communion. In Christ their Head "the Heavenly Father has gathered his elect together, and has joined them to himself by an indissoluble bond."[22] This constitutes the significant basis for Calvin's doctrine of the church.

Particular election—the election of individual persons to salvation—was so clearly taught by Calvin that it became the occasion for the common objection that God was then a respecter of persons. After some preliminary reflection on the real issue involved in this objection, Calvin presented his answer. The answer is a simple assertion of the Creator's sovereign right over His entire creation. There is nothing in human persons that accounts for their election or reprobation as such. The elect to whom God shows mercy are as guilty as the reprobate. Although the reprobate are eventually con-

---

to say that Esau was *first* elect in the choosing of all the descendants of Abraham, *then* rejected when Jacob was blessed." *The Knowledge of God*, p. 212 (italics added). It would be more accurate and true to Calvin to say that Esau was elect in the sense that he was a member of the elect nation, but at the same time he was not individually or personally elect unto salvation. In this latter sense Esau was always reprobate. See also Dowey, *The Knowledge of God*, p. 39; and Jacobs, *Prädestination*, pp. 57ff.

20. Ibid., 3.21.7 (OS, 4:377). Italics added. The Latin is *"ad singulas personas."*

21. Ibid.

22. Ibid. Cf. also 3.21.1 and especially 4.1, 12.

demned for their sins, the sovereign action of God in passing them by (preterition) was not occasioned by their sin.

Calvin's answer echoes Augustine: "Because God metes out merited penalty to those whom he condemns but distributes unmerited grace to those whom he calls, he is freed of all accusation—like a lender, who has the power of remitting payment to one, of exacting it from another."[23] And with Augustine, Calvin said: "The Lord can therefore also give grace . . . to whom he will . . . because he is merciful, and not give to all because he is a just judge. For by giving to some what they do not deserve, . . . he can show his free grace. . . . By not giving to all, he can manifest what all deserve."[24]

Abraham's heirs were not more worthy than other people when the nation of Israel was elected; likewise individuals elected unto salvation are no more worthy of election than are those rejected. It is due simply to God's sovereignty: "God chooses some, and passes over others according to his own decision. . . ."[25] "God has always been free to bestow his grace on whom he wills"; if anyone seeks a further cause than God's free sovereignty, "let them answer why they are men rather than oxen or asses. Although it was in God's power to make them dogs, he formed them in his own image."[26] Calvin's only response to such questions is the response of Paul: "But who are you, O man, to talk back to God? 'Shall what is formed say to him who formed it, "Why did you make me like this?"'" (Rom. 9:20 NIV).

From the above it ought to be clear what Calvin meant when he defined predestination as "God's eternal decree, by which he determined with himself what he willed to become of *each man*."[27] The decree of election makes a distinction between individuals where there is none by nature: in Jacob and Esau "all things are equal, yet God's judgment of each is different. For he receives one and rejects the other. . . . Disowning Ishmael, he sets his heart on Isaac [Gen. 21:12]. Setting Manasseh aside, he honors Ephraim

23. Ibid., 3.23.11 (OS, 4:405).

24. Ibid. See *Institutes*, p. 959 (note 26).

25. Ibid., 3.22.1 (OS, 4:380).

26. Ibid. Cf. 3.24.17 and also comments on Malachi 1:2–6.

27. Ibid., 3.21.5 (OS, 4:374). Italics added. See chap. 1, note 58 above.

more [Gen. 48:20]."[28] The decree is not known to men, however, except in rare instances when God chooses to reveal it. In the unique case of Jacob and Esau, the parents were told of God's eternal decree concerning their twins prior to their birth; Rebecca was divinely informed of the election of her son Jacob.[29] But even in this unique instance, this divine revelation did not become the basis for divergent action on the part of the parents. The means of grace were not to be withheld from Esau and given only to the elect Jacob.[30] The sovereign election of individuals to receive the gift of salvation through Jesus Christ emphasizes, however, the free mercy of God in giving to one what He withholds from another— and giving generously where no merit is present in the recipient.

The Cause and Ground of Election

The preceding section demonstrated that Calvin saw the salvation of believers rooted in the eternal and immutable decree of God. Now the question must be considered, Does that divine decree have some reason or cause as its basis? Why did God elect some persons and not others? Was it because of their good works? Or was it because He foreknew or foresaw their good works? These were not live options for Calvin. But others have presented such answers, and Calvin was forced to consider them. He emphatically denied good works or foreknowledge of them as reason or cause for God's decree of election. The first cause, the principal cause, the highest reason, the foundation of our election, according to Calvin, is God Himself—His sovereign will, His good pleasure. Thus the sovereignty of God stands out again in considering the cause and ground of election. Since works are not the basis for election, the gratuitous mercy of God also emerges prominently in the discussion. God chooses His elect in Christ: He, Jesus Christ, is the ground

---

28. Ibid., 3.22.5 (OS, 4:385).

29. "Rebecca, assured by divine oracle of the choice of her son Jacob, obtains the blessing for him by a wicked subterfuge [Gen. 27:9]." Ibid., 3.2.31 (OS, 4:41).

30. Contentions that the white race is elect or that the elect must rule the nonelect are caricatures of this doctrine and have absolutely no basis in Calvin's writings.

of their election. These features of Calvin's discussion must now be considered in some detail.

The cause is not good works. Calvin enumerated three reasons for rejecting the position that good works are the cause of the decree of election.[31] God made His decrees before the foundation of the world, so the persons elected did not yet exist to perform any works; all men are lost in Adam and hence incapable of performing any good works; finally, election is itself unto good works—"For he chose us in him before the creation of the world to be holy and blameless in his sight."[32]

The time of our election, therefore, proved for Calvin that it is purely gratuitous. "By saying that they were 'elect before the creation of the world' [Eph. 1:4], he takes away all regard for worth. For what basis for distinction is there among those who did not yet exist, and who were subsequently to be equals in Adam?"[33] Paul stated this specifically in another passage when he drew out the antithesis implied in Ephesians: God "has saved us and called us to a holy life—*not because of anything we have done* but because of his own purpose and grace."[34] But it is in Romans 9 "where Paul both reiterates this argument more profoundly and pursues it more at length."[35] There Paul said that the sovereign election of God made the distinction between Jacob and Esau and between believing and unbelieving Israel. "If their own piety established some in the hope of salvation, and their own desertion disinherited others, it would be quite absurd for Paul to lift his readers to secret election."[36]

The cause is not foreknowledge of works. What about God's foreknowledge of works? Is that not the cause and ground of election? Calvin's response was negative: "But though they had not yet

---

31. *Institutes* 3.22.3–4 (OS, 4:382ff.).

32. Eph. 1:4 (NIV), cited in ibid., 3.22.2 (OS, 4:381).

33. Ibid., 3.22.2 (OS, 4:381). See also *Ephesians* (on 1:4).

34. II Tim. 1:9 (NIV), cited in *Institutes* 3.22.3. Italics added.

35. Ibid., 3.22.4 (OS, 4:383).

36. Ibid.

acted, a certain sophist of the Sorbonne might reply, 'God foresaw what they could do.' This objection has no force in the nature of corrupt men, in whom nothing can be seen but materials for destruction."[37] "We are all lost in Adam; and therefore, had not God rescued us from perishing by His own election, there was nothing to be forseen."[38] Again Romans 9 rendered the decisive word for Calvin: "If foreknowledge had any bearing upon the distinction between the brothers, the mention of time would surely have been inopportune."[39] Calvin considered the various theories of Ambrose, Origen, Jerome, and Thomas,[40] but he rejected all on similar Scriptural grounds. If works were in any sense the basis for election, Paul could easily have overcome the charge that there was unrighteousness in God's discrimination by referring to them: "Paul could have settled this in one word, by proposing a regard for works. Why, then, does he not do this but rather continues a discourse that is fraught with the same difficulty? Why but because he ought not? For the Holy Spirit, speaking through his mouth, did not suffer from the fault of forgetfulness. Therefore he answers without circumlocutions: God shows favor to his elect because he so wills; he has mercy upon them because he so wills."[41] Therefore, "those who assign God's election to merits are wiser than they ought to be," as an ancient "ecclesiastical writer truly wrote."[42] Augustine's words also remain true: "God's grace does not find but makes those fit to be chosen."[43] "Finally," said Calvin, "from the words *election* and *purpose* it is certain that all causes that men commonly devise apart from God's secret plan are remote from this cause."[44]

The cause is God's sovereign will. The cause and ground of

---

37. *Ephesians* (on 1:4). OC, 51:147.

38. Ibid.

39. *Institutes* 3.22.4 (OS, 4:383).

40. Ibid., 3.22.8–9 (OS, 4:388ff.).

41. Ibid., 3.22.8 (OS, 4:389).

42. Ibid., 3.22.9 (OS, 4:390).

43. Ibid., 3.22.8 (OS, 4:389).

44. Ibid., 3.22.4 (OS, 4:384).

election cannot be human good works nor even God's foreknowledge of them. What then is election's ground? Calvin said that the only cause that can be named is simply the sovereign will of God. Jacob and Esau constitute Scripture's clearest example. "Esau and Jacob are brothers, born of the same parents, as yet enclosed in the same womb, not yet come forth into the light. In them all things are equal, yet God's judgment of each is different. For he receives one and rejects the other."[45] "Hence it ought not to be doubted that Jacob was, with the angels, engrafted into the body of Christ that he might share the same life. Jacob, therefore, is chosen and distinguished from the rejected Esau by God's predestination, while not differing from him in merits."[46] Or when Paul said in Ephesians 1:5, 9, that "God purposed in himself," this means "that he considered nothing outside himself with which to be concerned in making his decree. . . . Surely the grace of God deserves alone to be proclaimed in our election only if it is freely given. Now it will not be freely given if God, in choosing his own, considers what the works of each shall be."[47] If you ask for a reason for the distinction between Jacob and Esau, no other answer is permissible than God's own word to Moses: "I will have mercy on whom I have mercy, and I will have compassion on whom I have compassion."[48]

What is then the cause or reason for the decree of election? Paul gave the answer in Ephesians 1:5—"his pleasure and will" (NIV). If one attempts to push beyond the good pleasure of God's will, Calvin warned: ". . . it is very wicked merely to investigate the causes of God's will. For his will is, and rightly ought to be, the cause of all things that are."[49] "The everlasting decree of God . . . hath no causes whatsoever. . . . For God will have us use such soberness, that his bare will (*sa simple volonté*) may suffice us for all reasons. . . . It is wisdom in us to do whatever God appointed and never ask why."[50] Calvin himself followed that injunction in his

---

45. Ibid., 3.22.5 (OS, 4:384).

46. Ibid., 3.22.6 (OS, 4:385).

47. Ibid., 3.22.2 (OS, 4:382).

48. Rom. 9:15 (NIV). OC, 49:181–82. Cf. *Institutes* 3.22.6.

49. *Institutes* 3.23.2 (OS, 4:395f.).

50. On II Tim. 1:8–9. *Sermons on the Epistles of S. Paule to Timothie and Titus*, p. 703a (OC, 54:48).

1562 *Confession of Faith,* which was sent to the Diet at Frankfurt in the name of the French Reformed Churches: "We hold that the goodness which he displays towards us proceeds from his having elected us before the creation of the world, not seeking the cause of so doing out of himself and his good pleasure."[51] This emphasis upon God's sovereign will is not identical with the late–Middle Age concept of God as absolute power.[52] For Calvin the will of God is characterized by all of God's attributes; His will is just and holy and righteous. We shall consider this further when discussing God's will in connection with reprobation.

The ground is Christ. Calvin emphasized that sovereign election unto salvation is "election in Christ." Election stems from God's sovereign will, but there is a just basis or ground for this election. "When Paul teaches that we were chosen in Christ 'before the creation of the world' [Eph. 1:4a], he takes away all consideration of the real worth on our part, for it is just as if he said: since among all the offspring of Adam, the Heavenly Father found nothing worthy of his election, he turned his eyes upon his Anointed, to choose from that body as members those whom he was to take into the fellowship of life."[53]

Again in a later section Calvin said: "Accordingly, those whom God has adopted as his sons are said to have been chosen not in themselves but in his Christ [Eph. 1:4]; for unless he could love them in him, he could not honor them with the inheritance of his Kingdom if they had not previously become partakers of him."[54]

Election in Christ in no way minimized or altered the decretive character of divine election for Calvin. On the contrary, election in Christ sets forth the ground of this eternal divine decree, or its "material cause,"[55] as he called it in the Ephesian commentary.

---

51. Article 9. *Tracts and Treatises,* 2:142 (OC, 9:756).

52. Cf. *Institutes* 3.23.2. See chap. 3, note 37 below.

53. Ibid., 3.22.1 (OS, 4:380f.).

54. Ibid., 3.24.5 (OS, 4:415). Cf. Calvin in the *Articles Concerning Predestination:* "While we are elected in Christ, nevertheless that God reckons us among his own is prior in order to making us members of Christ." In *Theological Treatises,* p. 179 (OC, 9:714).

55. *Ephesians* (on 1:5). OC, 51:148.

Election in Christ does not minimize the sovereignty of the decree, but it does magnify the gratuitousness, the free mercy, of election. Election in Christ is a second proof[56] of the freedom of election: "When he adds, *In Christ*, it is the second confirmation of the freedom of election. For if we are chosen in Christ, it is outside ourselves. It is not from the sight of our deserving, but because our heavenly Father has engrafted us, through the blessing of adoption, into the Body of Christ. In short, the name of Christ excludes all merit, and everything which men have of themselves; for when he says that we are chosen in Christ, it follows that in ourselves we are unworthy."[57]

In opposing the "puerile fiction" of Pighius, Calvin provided a good summary of the significance of our election in Christ. He quoted John 6:37: "All that the Father gives me will come to me, and whoever comes to me I will never drive away" (NIV). According to Calvin we have here "three things briefly but clearly expressed": ". . . first, all that come to Christ were given to Him by the Father before; second, all who were given are transmitted from the Father's hand to His, so that they may be truly His; and lastly, He is a faithful custodian of all whom the Father entrusted to His good faith and protection, so that none is allowed to perish. Now if the question of the beginning of faith be raised, Christ replies: Those who believe believe because they were given to Him by the Father."[58]

The Goal and Means of Election

The goal is God's glory and our sanctification. The goal of God's eternal election is twofold. One goal Calvin called the final cause or ultimate design of election, namely, the glory of God. The other he called its proximate end, which is our sanctification. Commenting on the words of Ephesians 1:4, "to be holy and blameless in his

---

56. The first proof stemmed from the time of the decree—before the foundation of the world. *Ephesians* (on 1:4).

57. *Ephesians* (on 1:4). OC, 51:147.

58. *Eternal Predestination*, p. 72 (OC, 8:273). Cf. also Calvin on John 6 in *Institutes* 3.22.7.

sight" (NIV), Calvin said: "He indicates the immediate, but not the chief design. For there is no absurdity in supposing that one thing may have two objects. The design of building is that there should be a house. This is the immediate aim. But the convenience of dwelling in it is the ultimate aim. It was necessary to mention this in passing; for Paul at once mentions another aim, the glory of God. But there is no contradiction here. The glory of God is the highest end, to which our sanctification is subordinate."[59] In Ephesians 1:6 the phrase "to the praise of his glorious grace" (NIV) refers to the final cause of God's election. That appears again in verse 12, "for the praise of his glory" (NIV): "He repeats the purpose. For only then does God's glory shine in us, if we are nothing but vessels of His mercy. The word *glory* denotes, κατ᾽ ἐξοχήν, peculiarly that which shines in the goodness of God; for there is nothing more His own, in which He desires to be glorified, than His goodness."[60]

The glory of God was the unique emphasis of Calvin, both for his teaching and his own personal life. "*Soli Deo gloria!*" was his well-known motto. His comments on Ephesians are clear on this feature of election, but he did elaborate on it in his discussion of election in the *Institutes*. It is, however, as we have seen above, one of the pleasant fruits that comes from a right understanding of this doctrine. This perspective underlies his entire discussion of the sovereign and gratuitous mercy of God displayed in divine election.

In the *Institutes* Calvin gave much more attention to the immediate goal of election—our sanctification—and to questions relating to this goal. The immediate goal of election is the sanctification of the elect—to make them "holy and blameless in his sight" (Eph. 1:4 NIV)—and that sanctification leads the believer to glorify his sovereign, gracious Lord. Sovereign election provides all the means to attain the total goal of God's sovereign purpose. Romans 8:29–30 provides the basic structure for these means by which God effectuates His eternal election, namely, calling, justification, glorification. There is a reciprocal action; the means direct attention to God's source and goal: "Now among the elect we regard the call

---

59. *Ephesians* (on 1:4). OC, 51:147.
60. Ibid., 1:12 (OC, 51:152).

as a testimony of election. Then we hold justification another sign of its manifestation, until they come into the glory in which the fulfillment of that election lies."[61] This also indicates the crucial significance of the doctrine of election for the whole of Calvin's theology. Election envelops the whole redemptive process from the eternal decree to its final accomplishment in glory. Between these poles election is relevant to the doctrine of faith, the knowledge of God, the whole of soteriology, and the church and sacraments, and to eschatology as well.[62] Thus Calvin finally found the right place for his discussion of predestination—book 3, which deals largely with soteriology. Soteriology culminates in eschatology; for "the steadfast love of the Lord is from everlasting to everlasting upon those who fear him" (Ps. 103:17 RSV). Calvin quoted Bernard with approval on this perspective: "From everlasting because of predestination, to everlasting because of beatification—the one knowing no beginning, the other no end."[63]

The means is preaching. God makes use of means to bring His decreed goal to realization. And these very means are also included in God's decree and are under His sovereign control. By divine command the gospel must be preached to all people; yet not all hear, and among those who do, responses differ.[64] God's predestination is involved. "Even though the preaching of the gospel streams forth from the wellspring of election, because such preaching is shared also with the wicked, it cannot of itself be a full proof of election."[65] The calling that is proof of election, the calling referred to in Romans 8:30, "consists not only in the preaching of the Word but also in the illumination of the Spirit."[66] This effective calling is

---

61. *Institutes* 3.21.7 (OS, 4:379).

62. Ibid., 3.21.1. See also Polman, *De praedestinatieleer*, pp. 357–77; Torrance, *Calvin's Doctrine of Man*, pp. 105, 107; and Heinrich Quistorp, *Calvin's Doctrine of the Last Things*, p. 24. Quistorp spoke of election and eschatology as twin doctrines.

63. Ibid., 3.22.10 (OS, 4:392).

64. Ibid., 3.21.1 (OS, 4:368f.).

65. Ibid., 3.21.1 (OS, 4:410). This was added in the 1559 edition.

66. Ibid., 3.24.2 (OS, 4:412).

one of the means of election: "Although in choosing his own the Lord already has adopted them as his children, we see that they do not come into possession of so great a good except when they are called; conversely, that when they are called, they already enjoy some share of their election."[67]

Does the universal call of the gospel then conflict with particular election? If not, what is its real significance? Calvin faced these questions boldly, carefully, and Scripturally. He frankly stated that the universality of the promise does not destroy the distinction of special grace.[68] We may *not* say that the gospel is "effectually profitable to all."[69] If God "willed all to be saved, he would set his Son over them, and would engraft all into his body with the sacred bond of faith. Now it is certain that faith is a singular pledge of the Father's love, reserved for the sons whom he has adopted."[70]

These considerations do not mean that the preaching of the gospel to all is meaningless.

> It is easy to explain why the general election of a people is not always firm and effectual: to those with whom God makes a covenant, he does not at once give the spirit of regeneration that would enable them to persevere in the covenant to the very end. Rather, the outward change without the working of inner grace, which might have availed to keep them, is *intermediate* between the rejection of mankind and the election of a meager number of the godly.[71]

Relying upon Augustine, Calvin explained how the gospel should be preached:

> If anyone addresses the people in this way: "If you do not believe, the reason is that you have already been divinely destined for destruction," he not only fosters sloth but also

---

67. Ibid., 3.24.1 (OS, 4:410).

68. Ibid., 3.22.10 (OS, 4:390).

69. Ibid., 3.22.10 (OS, 4:391). The Latin is *"ut efficaciter prosit."*

70. Ibid., 3.22.10 (OS, 4:392).

71. Ibid., 3.21.7 (OS, 4:378). Italics added. The Latin is *"medium quiddam est."* For the words "without the working of inner grace," the Latin has *"absque interiori gratiae efficacia."*

gives place to evil intention. If anyone extends to the future also the statement that they who hear will not believe because they have been condemned, this will be cursing rather than teaching. . . . "For as we know not who belongs to the number of the predestined or who does not belong, we ought to be so minded as to wish that all men be saved." So shall it come about that we try to make every one we meet a sharer in our peace. . . . It belongs to God, however, to make that rebuke useful to those whom he . . . has foreknown and predestined.[72]

At the same time Calvin held that the preaching of the gospel, even for the reprobate, involves a display of God's "great benefit,"[73] or common grace. A heavier judgment therefore awaits the reprobate who have heard the gospel and rejected it than those who lived before the coming of Christ and never heard the gospel.[74]

The preaching of the gospel is primarily a means for effectuating the decree of election. That is why Calvin referred to gospel preaching as streaming "forth from the wellspring of election."[75] He explained: "The elect are gathered into Christ's flock by a call not immediately at birth, and not all at the same time, but according as it pleases God to dispense his grace to them. But before they are gathered unto that supreme Shepherd, they wander scattered in the wilderness common to all; and they do not differ at all from others except that they are protected by God's especial mercy from rushing headlong into the final ruin of death."[76] This inner call stems from the "free goodness" of God and results from "the effectual working of his Spirit"; hence, "this inner call . . . is a pledge of salvation that cannot deceive us."[77]

Calvin suggested that especially two errors need to be avoided in

72. Ibid., 3.23.14 (OS, 4:409f.).

73. Ibid., 3.24.12 (OS, 4:396). Cf. Herman Kuiper, *Calvin on Common Grace.*

74. Ibid., 3.24.12–13.

75. Ibid., 3.24.1 (OS, 4:410).

76. Ibid., 3.24.10 (OS, 4:421). Cf. 3.24.11: ". . . he only preserves them from falling into unpardonable blasphemy."

77. Ibid., 3.24.2 (OS, 4:412). "*Interior igitur haec vocatio pignus est salutis quod fallere non potest.*"

understanding the relation of election and faith. First is the error of some who "make man God's co-worker, to ratify election by his consent," for this makes "man's will superior to God's plan."[78] Scripture does not say that we are "merely given the ability to believe"; it states that we are given "faith itself."[79] The second error is that of regarding election as dependent upon faith, "as if it were doubtful and also ineffectual until confirmed by faith."[80] According to Calvin "it is false to say that election takes effect only after we have embraced the gospel, and takes its validity from this."[81] He did admit of course that election is "confirmed, with respect to us," for "the secret plan of God, which lay hidden, is brought to light, provided you understand by this language merely that what was unknown is now verified—sealed, as it were, with a seal."[82] The presence of true faith is also a ground for our assurance of God's election. While the inner, effectual call confirms election, we must not confuse cause and effect. The pipe through which the water flows to us must not be confused with the fountain from which that water springs.[83] Thus Calvin said that "faith is fitly joined to election, provided it takes second place."[84] Election is the parent of faith. God employs calling, faith, justification, and sanctification as the means for accomplishing the glorification decreed from eternity. "The Lord seals his elect by call and justification"; therefore, Calvin said: "Now among the elect we regard the call as a testimony of election. Then we hold justification another sign of its manifestation, until they come into the glory in which the fulfillment of that election lies."[85]

In this light we understand Calvin's refutation of the objection that his doctrine of predestination removes all incentive for respon-

---

78. Ibid., 3.24.3 (OS, 4:413).

79. Ibid.

80. Ibid.

81. Ibid.

82. Ibid.

83. Ibid.

84. Ibid., 3.22.10 (OS, 4:392).

85. Ibid., 3.21.7 (OS, 4:379).

sible ethical activity.[86] Calvin admitted that some people had polluted the doctrine of predestination with such foul blasphemy, but he recalled the words of Paul, that we have been elected in Christ "to be holy and blameless in his sight."[87] "If election has as its goal holiness of life, it ought rather to arouse and goad us eagerly to set our mind upon it than to serve as a pretext for doing nothing."[88] Sadoleto was one who charged that Calvin's doctrine of predestination led to indolence; Calvin's reply is indicative of the way he treated this objection:

> Since therefore, according to us, Christ regenerates to a blessed life those whom he justifies, and after rescuing them from the dominion of sin, hands them over to the dominion of righteousness, transforms them into the image of God, and so trains them by his Spirit into obedience to his will, there is no ground to complain that by our doctrine, lust is left with loosened reins. . . . Nay rather, as the end of gratuitous election, so also of gratuitous justification is, that we may lead pure and unpolluted lives before God. For the saying of Paul is true (I Thess. 4:7), we have not been called to impurity but to holiness.[89]

Knowledge of our election is based on Christ. But how does one know he is elect? Calvin asked that question too: "Now, what revelation do you have of your election?"[90] That question arises in almost everyone who reflects upon election as the source of salvation. Satan deviously tries to unsettle us. Calvin contended that "Satan has no more grievous or dangerous temptation to dishearten believers than when he unsettles them with doubt about their election, while at the same time he arouses them with a wicked desire to seek it outside the way."[91] The desire for security is not itself the temptation; the temptation is to seek security in an improper way.

---

86. Ibid., 3.23.12–14 (OS, 4:405ff.).

87. Eph. 1:4 in ibid., 3.22.3 (OS, 4:382).

88. Ibid., 3.23.12 (OS, 4:406).

89. *Reply to Sadoleto,* in *Tracts and Treatises,* 1:43f. (OC, 5:398–99).

90. *Institutes* 3.24.4 (OS, 4:414). *"Electionis porro quae tibi revelatio?"*

91. Ibid.

Calvin said: "I call it 'seeking outside the way' when mere man attempts to break into the inner recesses of divine wisdom, and tries to penetrate even to the highest eternity, in order to find out what decision has been made concerning himself at God's judgment seat."[92] If a man attempts to do that, "he casts himself into the depths of a bottomless whirlpool to be swallowed up; then he tangles himself in innumerable and inextricable snares; then he buries himself in an abyss of sightless darkness."[93] To suffer shipwreck on that rock means the loss of "peace and tranquillity toward God."[94]

It is in connection with the quest for certainty regarding one's election that Calvin referred to Jesus Christ as the mirror of election.[95] First, we should recall Calvin's emphasis upon our election in Christ, for this is closely related to Christ as the mirror of election:

> Accordingly, those whom God has adopted as his sons are said to have been chosen not in themselves but in his Christ [Eph. 1:4]; for unless he could love them in him, he could not honor them with the inheritance of his Kingdom if they had not previously become partakers of him. But if we have been chosen in him, we shall not find assurance of our election in ourselves; and not even in God the Father, if we conceive him as severed from his Son. Christ, then, is the mirror wherein we must, and without self-deception may, contemplate our own election. For since it is into his body the Father has destined those to be engrafted whom he has willed from eternity to be his own, that he may hold as sons all whom he acknowledges to be among his members, we have

---

92. Ibid.

93. Ibid.

94. Ibid.

95. In a few instances Calvin used the figure of the mirror in relation to Christ in another sense. Cf. *Institutes* 3.22.1 (OS, 4:380). Here the idea of gracious election in its sovereign character is seen in the election of Christ, who "is conceived a mortal man of the seed of David" to be made "head of the angels," etc. Calvin used the idea of the mirror in a variety of ways. This sense of Christ as the elect is radically different from Karl Barth's view.

a sufficiently clear and firm testimony that we have been inscribed in the book of life [cf. Rev. 21:27] if we are in communion with Christ.[96]

We should turn our eyes to Christ for security. For "what is the purpose of election but that we, adopted as sons by our Heavenly Father, may obtain salvation and immortality by his favor?"[97] Assurance of election does not come from some special revelation; nor does it come from curious attempts to pry into the eternal decree of God. Christ is the mirror, and "if we desire anything more than to be reckoned among God's sons and heirs, we have to rise above Christ. If this is our ultimate goal, how insane are we to seek outside him what we have already obtained in him, and can find in him alone?"[98] "Therefore, if we desire to know whether God cares for our salvation, let us inquire whether he has entrusted us to Christ, whom he has established as the sole Savior of all his people."[99] This is what Calvin meant when he said that "the firmness of our election is joined to our calling";[100] hence to acquire "the inestimable fruit of comfort" and assurance, the Word requires that we "begin with God's call, and . . . end with it."[101]

Looking to Christ as the mirror of our election may give assurance for the present, but what about the future? Some people seem to have true faith and appear to be joined to Christ; yet they fall away later. Calvin also faced this problem. For the future also Christ is the mirror of election and assurance for our perseverance (preservation). "But Christ has freed us from this anxiety, for these promises surely apply to the future: 'All that the Father gives me will come to me; and him who will come to me I will not cast out' [John 6:37]."[102] Calvin mentioned other passages and concluded

---

96. *Institutes* 3.24.5 (OS, 4:415f.).

97. Ibid. (OS, 4:415).

98. Ibid. (OS, 4:416).

99. Ibid., 3.24.6 (OS, 4:417).

100. Ibid. (OS, 4:416).

101. Ibid., 3.24.4 (OS, 4:415).

102. Ibid., 3.24.6 (OS, 4:417). Calvin referred to John 6:37, 39; 10:27–28; Matt. 15:13; I John 2:19; Rom. 8:38; Phil. 1:6; Luke 22:32.

with the question: "What did Christ wish to have us learn from this but to trust that we shall ever remain safe because we have been made his once for all?"[103] Since Christ is "the eternal wisdom of the Father, his unchangeable truth, his firm counsel, we ought not to be afraid of what he tells us in his Word varying in the slightest from that will of the Father which we seek. Rather, he faithfully reveals to us that will as it was from the beginning and ever shall be."[104] Christ must be taken at His word; these promises are so certain that it is not permissible for the believer to pray, "O Lord, if I have been chosen, hear me."[105] That formulation indicates doubt in the promises of God. Scripture does indicate that some who seem to belong to Christ will later fall away. Calvin explained that "it is also equally plain that such persons never cleaved to Christ with the heartfelt trust in which certainty of election has, I say, been established for us."[106] He continued: "So then, let not such instances induce us at all to abandon a quiet reliance upon the Lord's promise, where he declares that all by whom he is received in true faith have been given to him by the Father, no one of whom, since he is their guardian and shepherd, will perish [cf. John 3:16; 6:39]."[107]

Calvin's reference to Christ as the mirror of our election is a good example of the Biblical way in which he avoided frigid speculation. It is equally important to observe, contrary to some interpreters, that Calvin did not introduce the so-called *syllogismus practicus*.[108] True, the line between what Calvin did and the practical syllogism is razor thin; but Calvin did not urge people to look at their own good works to find confidence in themselves. His clear emphasis is upon the work of Christ performed in believers. He did say that in seeking the certainty of our election, we should "cling to those latter signs which are sure attestations of it."[109] But here

---

103. Ibid.

104. Ibid., 3.24.5 (OS, 4:416).

105. Ibid.

106. Ibid., 3.24.7 (OS, 4:418).

107. Ibid.

108. See Karl Barth, *Die kirchliche Dogmatik*, 2 (part 2): 369; *Church Dogmatics*, 2 (part 2): 335f. Cf. Wilhelm Niesel, *The Theology of Calvin*, pp. 170ff., 175ff.

109. *Institutes* 3.24.4 (OS, 4:414). *"In iis signis posterioribus."*

Calvin was contrasting these "latter signs" with the futile attempt to look into the prior eternal counsel and decree of God. When he elaborated upon these "latter signs," he never emphasized the believer's good works. It is Christ's work and His promises that are evident in these "latter signs."

One need only review the quotations cited above: "Christ, then, is the mirror wherein we must, and without self-deception may, contemplate our own election."[110] Again, "If we desire to know whether God cares for our salvation, let us inquire whether he has entrusted us to Christ. . . ."[111] So too with regard to future assurance, the focus is not in the security that resides in ourselves but in that which is rooted in the promises of Christ. The calling, which according to Calvin should be the beginning and end of our examination of this question, is the calling of God that "consists not only in the preaching of the Word but also in the illumination of the Spirit."[112] In his tract *Concerning the Eternal Predestination of God*, Calvin pointedly summarized the *Institutes* on this matter: "Confidence of salvation is founded upon Christ and rests on the promises of the gospel."[113] This is not a *syllogismus practicus*, which draws logical conclusions from the believer's good works.

Calvin's insistence that Christ is the mirror of election in no way minimizes the decretive character of eternal election. Rather, the reference to Christ as the mirror is firmly rooted in the eternal decree of God whereby we were elected in Christ. When Calvin warned against futile attempts to penetrate the hidden counsel of God in search of assurance and certainty of one's election, he in no way wished to leave the impression that there is no eternal decree of election.[114] The question is actually how one can come to *know* about this eternal decree and be assured of his election. Calvin

---

110. Ibid., 3.24.5 (OS, 4:415).

111. Ibid., 3.24.6 (OS, 4:417).

112. Ibid., 3.24.2 (OS, 4:412).

113. *Eternal Predestination*, p. 56 (OC, 8:260). "*In Christo fundata est salutis fiducia, et in evangeli promissiones recumbit.*"

114. Cf. also ibid., pp. 126ff. (OC, 8:318ff.). Torrance (in *Calvin's Doctrine of Man*) and Dowey (in *The Knowledge of God*) left the opposite impression.

answered that we have no direct access to the decree or counsel of God. We can know it only indirectly, though truly and certainly, from the work of Christ in and for us. For those who wish it "put more bluntly," Calvin explained that "election is prior to faith, but is learnt by faith." He said further:

> Therefore Christ, when commending the eternal election of His own in the counsel of His Father, at the same time shows where their faith may rest secure. I have manifested, He says (John 17:6), Thy name to the men whom Thou didst give Me. Thine they were, and Thou didst give them to Me, and they have kept Thy word. We see here that God begins with Himself when He sees fit to elect us; but He will have us begin with Christ so that we may know that we are reckoned among His peculiar people.[115]

In one of his sermons Calvin also urged his hearers to recognize that "the grace of Jesus Christ" is joined "with the everlasting counsel of God the Father."[116] He encouraged his hearers to seek assurance of their election by contemplating the calling and faith rooted in Jesus Christ. At the same time Calvin warned that they must not lose sight of God's eternal decree: "But we must here remark, that when we have knowledge of our salvation, when God hath called us and enlightened us in the faith of his gospel, it is not to bring to nought the everlasting predestination that went before."[117]

In summary, Calvin emphasized God's sovereign, gratuitous election. God's eternal decree is sovereign, and its righteous ground is the grace of Jesus Christ. Our knowledge of the decree is based on Christ as the mirror of election, according to the whole of Scripture. Understood in this Biblical way, the doctrine of election provides peace and security for the true believer, and election issues in the rich fruit of Christian comfort. The following words of Calvin provide a fitting conclusion for this section: "Even though

---

115. *Eternal Predestination*, p. 127 (OC, 8:318–19).

116. On II Tim. 1:9–10. *Sermons on Timothie and Titus*, p. 708b (OC, 54:54).

117. Ibid., p. 710a. Cf. also pp. 706–8.

discussion about predestination is likened to a dangerous sea, still, in traversing it, one finds safe and calm—I also add pleasant—sailing unless he willfully desire to endanger himself. For just as those engulf themself in a deadly abyss who, to make their election more certain, investigate God's eternal plan apart from his Word, so those who rightly and duly examine it as it is contained in his Word reap the inestimable fruit of comfort."[118]

---

118. *Institutes* 3.24.4 (OS, 4:414f.).

CHAPTER 3

Sovereign and
Just Reprobation

P R O B A B L Y N O O N E knew better than Calvin himself that the doctrine of double predestination is not popular. "Now when human understanding hears these things," he wrote, "its insolence is so irrepressible that it breaks forth into random and immoderate tumult as if at the blast of a battle trumpet." [1] Calvin was thinking of those who accepted election but denied reprobation. Some of Calvin's friends and even some fellow Reformers urged him to soft-pedal the doctrine of reprobation. [2] "Indeed many, as if they wished to avert a reproach from God, accept election in such terms as to deny that anyone is condemned," he observed. "But they do this very ignorantly and childishly," he added, "since election itself could not stand except as set over against reprobation." [3]

Calvin did not mean that reprobation is a logical deduction from the doctrine of election; he made the assertion above from the full conviction that Scripture requires it. "If we are not ashamed of the gospel, we must confess what is there plainly declared. God, by His eternal goodwill, which has no cause outside itself, destined those

---

1. *Institutes* 3.23.1 (OS, 4:393).

2. This was especially true when advice was sought from other Swiss cantons in connection with the Bolsec case. Cf. Andries D. R. Polman, *De praedestinatieleer van Augustinus, Thomas van Aquino en Calvijn: Een dogmahistorische studie*, pp. 341f.

3. *Institutes* 3.23.1 (OS, 4:394).

whom He pleased to salvation, rejecting the rest; those whom He dignified by gratuitous adoption He illumined by His Spirit, so that they receive the life offered in Christ, while others voluntarily disbelieve, so that they remain in darkness destitute of the light of faith." [4]

Calvin spoke openly of the "incomprehensible plan" of God and admitted that reprobation raises questions that he could not answer. He considered himself compelled to defend the doctrine of reprobation, however, because Scripture requires it. In reference to Romans 9, he said "that hardening is in God's hand and will, just as much as mercy is. . . . And Paul does not, as do those I have spoken of [that is, those who deny reprobation while affirming election], labor anxiously to make false excuses in God's defense; he only warns that it is unlawful for the clay to quarrel with its potter [Rom. 9:20]." [5]

In summarizing Calvin's doctrine of reprobation, we can employ the same divisions used in summarizing his doctrine of election—with one exception. Our discussion of Calvin's doctrine of "sovereign and just reprobation" will deal with the divine decree of reprobation, the cause (but not the ground) of reprobation, and its goal and means. Reprobation is as sovereign as election; however, Calvin emphasized the justice of God's sovereignty in reprobation, in contrast to the free grace of His sovereignty in election.

The Divine Decree of Reprobation

Calvin understood the eternal counsel of God as the expression of His sovereign will and purpose for the entire history of the world. History is the unfolding of this immutable counsel of God. God's foreknowledge, as well as His providence, is rooted in His eternal counsel. The decree of election is part of God's eternal counsel. Now we must follow Calvin's discussion of reprobation. Reproba-

---

4. *Concerning the Eternal Predestination of God*, p. 58 (OC, 8:261–62). Cf. 3.23.1.

5. *Institutes* 3.23.1 (OS, 4:394).

tion, as well as election, concerns the eternal decree or sovereign counsel of God. That is where Calvin's discussion begins.

Reprobation involves God's decretive work. A review of Calvin's definitions of predestination demonstrates that Calvin tied reprobation to God's eternal decree.

> We call predestination God's *eternal decree*, by which he compacted with himself what he willed to become of each man. For all are not created in equal condition; rather, eternal life is *foreordained* for some, *eternal damnation* for others. Therefore, as any man has been created to one or the other of these ends, we speak of him as *predestined* to life or *to death*.[6]

> As Scripture, then, clearly shows, we say that God once established by his *eternal and unchangeable plan* those whom he long before *determined* once for all to receive into salvation, and those whom, on the other hand, he would devote *to destruction*.[7]

> Jacob, therefore, is chosen and distinguished from the *rejected Esau* by God's *predestination*, while not differing from him in merits.[8]

These summaries of Calvin's view are clear. Reprobation concerns the *divine* decree. We should observe, however, that Calvin made no specific reference to the distinct persons of the Trinity in connection with reprobation as He did in connection with election. The work of God is of course the work of God Triune, as was observed earlier.[9] Calvin did not specifically repeat this in his discussion of reprobation. While Calvin said that the Son as well as the Father was the author of the decree of election, he made no such reference in connection with reprobation. That the Holy Spirit is the actual teacher of this doctrine of reprobation follows from

---

6. Ibid., 3.21.5 (OS, 4:374). Italics added. Cf. chap. 1, note 58 above.

7. Ibid., 3.21.7 (OS, 4:378). Italics added. Cf. chap. 1, note 59 above.

8. Ibid., 3.22.6 (OS, 4:385). Italics added.

9. See chap. 2, note 7 above.

Calvin's view of the inspiration of Scripture. He did make this specific when referring to those who reject this difficult doctrine: such people were not simply opposing him, but Paul and the Holy Spirit.[10]

Calvin also contended that this doctrine of reprobation had been clearly taught by Christ Himself. Calvin asked: "Now how will those who do not admit that any are condemned by God dispose of Christ's statement: 'Every tree that my . . . Father has not planted will be uprooted' [Matt. 15:13, paraphrase]?" And he added that "this plainly means that all those whom the Heavenly Father has not deigned to plant as sacred trees in his field are marked and intended for destruction. If they say this is no sign of reprobation, there is nothing so clear that it can be proved to them."[11]

Yet Calvin recognized that an appeal to one clear passage of Scripture would not stop the mouths of his opponents. Hence he again appealed to Romans: "Let readers note that Paul, to cut off occasion for whispering and disparagement, gives the ultimate sovereignty to God's wrath and might, for it is wicked to subject to our determination those deep judgments which swallow up all our powers of mind."[12] Calvin was referring to these words of Paul: "What if God, choosing to show his wrath and make his power known, bore with great patience the objects of his wrath— prepared for destruction? What if he did this to make the riches of his glory known to the objects of his mercy, whom he prepared in advance for glory. . . ?"[13] To the argument that the variation in the phrases "prepared for destruction" and "prepared in advance for glory" seem to take reprobation out of the eternal decree, Calvin responded: "But though I should admit to them [who so argue] that Paul, using a different expression, softens the harshness of the former clause, it is utterly inconsistent to transfer the preparation for destruction to anything but God's secret plan. This was also

---

10. *The Epistles of Paul the Apostle to the Romans and to the Thessalonians* (on Rom. 9:14). OC, 49:181. Cf. also *Brief Reply*, in *Theological Treatises*, p. 191 (OC, 9:258).

11. *Institutes* 3.23.1 (OS, 4:394).

12. Ibid.

13. Rom. 9:22–23 (NIV).

declared in a little earlier context: God aroused Pharaoh [Rom. 9:17]; then, 'he hardens whom he pleases' [Rom. 9:18]. From this it follows that God's secret plan is the cause of hardening." [14] Here Calvin was endorsing the interpretation of Augustine—"Where might is joined to long-suffering, God does not permit but governs by his power." [15] Although Calvin did not regularly use such distinctions as preterition and condemnation, which later Reformed theologians employed in discussing reprobation,[16] we do find these ideas distinguished in his discussion. We shall refer to this later when we consider sin in relation to God's decree.

Reprobation is particular. For Calvin, reprobation, like the decree of election, concerns specific individuals; election and reprobation are specific and particular. The decree of reprobation does not refer to a general intention of God; it is not limited in its reference to a class of people, as the later Arminians contended. The general definitions of predestination quoted above make this clear; so also do the specific references to Esau in distinction from Jacob. Only in the light of individual or particular reprobation could the problem arise that Calvin considered. That problem stems from the alleged inconsistency of the fact that "God is said to have ordained from eternity those whom he wills to embrace in love, and those upon whom he wills to vent his wrath," and the fact that God "announces salvation to all men indiscriminately." [17] Objectors challenge the justice of God precisely because God's decree concerns individuals.[18]

Although God's decree of reprobation clearly refers to individuals, Calvin insisted that we do not know who the reprobate are. This is known alone to God; hence we may never deal in history with any individual as if he or she were clearly reprobate.

---

14. *Institutes* 3.23.1 (OS, 4:395).

15. Ibid, 3.23.1 (OS, 4:394).

16. E.g., Louis Berkhof, *Systematic Theology*, p. 116. But note *Institutes* 3.23.1 (OS, 4:394). See note 32 below.

17. *Institutes* 3.24.17 (OS, 4:430).

18. Ibid., 3.23.2, 3. Cf. 3.21.7 (OS, 4:377) The Latin is *"ad singulas personas."*

We have the task to preach the gospel to all. We must also desire the salvation of all to whom we preach and need never fear that by so doing we contradict the will of God by which He sovereignly decreed to reprobate some.[19] Even when the church, obedient to the command of its Lord, finds it necessary to excommunicate a member, not even then is that person to be regarded as clearly reprobate, for such a person is "in the hand and judgment of God alone."[20] One of the intents of excommunication is to lead the sinner to repentance; for this the church must continue to pray.[21] Here too it is the teaching and example of the apostle Paul that Calvin echoed.

The Cause of Reprobation

We have seen that according to Calvin, reprobation as well as election concerns the eternal, unchangeable, and sovereign decree of God that relates to specific individuals. Now we must face the question of whether this divine decree has some cause outside God's will. Is God's decree to reprobate some individuals based upon their sinful actions? Or since the decree concerns persons who do not yet exist, is the foreknowledge of their sinful actions the cause of God's decree? Why the difference in God's decrees concerning Jacob and Esau? Calvin devoted a good deal of attention to such questions. In that context he also considered various objections that arise concerning foreknowledge, permission, and the relation of God to sin. Calvin's discussion of such problems makes this an appropriate place to deal with the question of the so-called equal ultimacy of election and reprobation.

The cause is not sin. When the question is raised of the cause of God's decree of reprobation, the most common answer is human sin. That appears to be the simplest and most obvious solution. Reference to human actions seems to be tenable with respect to

---

19. Ibid., 3.24.13, 14 (OS, 4:424ff.).

20. Ibid., 4.12.9 (OS, 5:220).

21. Ibid., 4.12.8, 9 (OS, 5:219ff.).

reprobation, in contrast to the cause of God's decree of election. Election is aimed at producing good works that glorify God; hence human works are excluded from consideration as the cause of God's decree of election. With respect to reprobation, however, the sinful actions of men and women are certainly related to the final condemnation that proceeds from a righteous God. Calvin repeatedly emphasized that no one is finally condemned who does not fully deserve that condemnation. The question now before us, however, is the cause not of a person's final condemnation, but of the divine decree itself. Calvin cannot be accurately understood if this distinction is not kept in mind. What is the cause of the eternal decree of reprobation according to Calvin? That is the question here.

Calvin emphatically contended that sinful works are not the cause or basis for God's eternal decree of reprobation. Paul and Romans 9 are crucial again for his argument. "For as Jacob, deserving nothing by good works, is taken into grace, so Esau, as yet undefiled by any crime, is hated [Rom. 9:13]."[22] "If we turn our eyes to works," Calvin immediately added, "we wrong the apostle, as if he did not see what is quite clear to us!"[23] Calvin continued: "Now it is proved that he did not see it, since he specifically emphasizes the point that when as yet they had done nothing good or evil, one was chosen, the other rejected. This is to prove that *the foundation of divine predestination is not in works.*"[24]

The cause is not foreknowledge of sin. Since the works here under consideration could not yet have been performed, the case for foreknowledge of such evil works as the basis for the decree of reprobation appears stronger. Calvin also weighed this possibility but rejected it on Biblical grounds. "But since he foresees future events only by reason of the fact that he decreed that they take place, they vainly raise a quarrel over foreknowledge, when it is clear that all things take place rather by his determination and

---

22. Ibid., 3.22.11 (OS, 4:393). The Latin is "*odio habetur.*"

23. Ibid. Cf. *Romans* (on 9:14). OC, 49:181.

24. *Institutes* 3.22.11. Italics added. ". . . *ut probet divinae praedestinatione fundamentum in operibus non esse.*"

bidding."[25] Calvin saw the solution to this problem in the correct understanding of the relation of foreknowledge, providence, and predestination. Reflecting upon Proverbs 16:4, Calvin wrote: "Behold! Since the disposition of all things is in God's hand, since the decision of salvation or of death rests in his power, he so ordains by his plan and will that among men some are born destined for certain death from the womb, who glorify his name by their own destruction. . . . Both life and death are acts of God's will more than of his foreknowledge."[26] Certainly God foreknew what will take place: he "not only *foreknew* it, but *ordained* it."[27] Hence foreknowledge cannot be considered the cause of the divine decree of reprobation.

The cause is God's sovereign will. If the decree of reprobation does not have its foundation in the sinful works of those reprobated or in the divine foreknowledge of such works, what is its foundation? Calvin's answer came from his analysis of Romans 9. Paul vigorously rejected the suspicion that there is unrighteousness with God. But he did not do so by appealing to Esau's sinful actions. When Paul "raised the objection, whether God is unjust, he does not make use of what would have been the surest and clearest defense of his righteousness: that God recompensed Esau according to his own evil intention."[28] Rather, Paul "contents himself with a different solution, that the reprobate are raised up to the end that through them God's glory may be revealed."[29] Paul concluded: "Therefore God has mercy on whom he wants to have mercy, and he hardens whom he wants to harden."[30] That led Calvin to conclude: "Do you see how Paul attributes both to God's decision alone? If, then, we cannot determine a reason why he vouchsafes mercy to his own, except that it so pleases him, neither shall we

---

25. Ibid., 3.23.6 (OS, 4:401).

26. Ibid. (OS, 4:400f.).

27. *Brief Reply*, in *Theological Treatises*, p. 199 (OC, 9:262).

28. *Institutes* 3.22.11 (OS, 4:393).

29. Ibid.

30. Rom. 9:18 (NIV).

have any reason for rejecting others, other than his will. For when it is said that God hardens or shows mercy to whom he wills, men are warned by this to seek no cause outside his will."[31] Calvin also expressed it this way: ". . . those whom God passes over (*praeterit*), he condemns (*reprobat*); and this he does for no other reason than that he wills to exclude them from the inheritance which he predestines (*praedestinat*) for his own children."[32] What is the cause of God's decree of reprobation? Calvin's answer is, the sovereign good pleasure of God. No cause other than His sovereign will can be adduced.[33]

Calvin's answer to this question occasioned various objections. If God's will alone is the cause of reprobation, why should He then object to the sinful actions of persons whom He reprobates? Does this answer not imply that God is the author of sin? Calvin considered such objections:

> Foolish men contend with God in many ways, as though they held him liable to their accusations. They first ask, therefore, by what right the Lord becomes angry at his creatures who have not provoked him by any previous offense; for to devote to destruction whomever he pleases is more like the caprice of a tyrant than the lawful sentence of a judge. It therefore seems to them that men have reason to expostulate with God if they are predestined to eternal death solely by his decision, apart from their own merit.[34]

The first thing Calvin said in response to that objection is a warning to believers: "If thoughts of this sort ever occur to pious men, they will be sufficiently armed to break their force even by the one consideration that it is very wicked merely to investigate the causes of God's will. For his will is, and rightly ought to be, the cause of

---

31. *Institutes* 3.22.11 (OS, 4:393). Cf. 3.23.1.

32. Ibid., 3.23.1 (OS, 4:394). Cf. *Romans* (on 9:11). OC, 49:177–79.

33. In this sense Calvin sometimes stated that no cause for the divine decree can be given, only thus reasserting the sovereignty of God's will. Cf. Rom. 9:14, 22.

34. *Institutes* 3.23.2 (OS, 4:395).

all things that are."[35] If the will of God has a cause, "something must precede it, to which it is, as it were, bound; this is unlawful to imagine."[36] Then in a remarkable section added to the final edition of the *Institutes*, Calvin indicated that his view of God's will is far different from that of some theologians of the late Middle Ages who held to "the fiction of 'absolute might.'" He labeled that view "profane," one the Christian should rightly hate: "We fancy no lawless god who is a law unto himself. For, as Plato says, men who are troubled with lusts are in need of law; but the will of God is not only free of all fault but is the highest rule of perfection, and even the law of all laws."[37] Earlier Calvin had put it this way: "For God's will is so much the highest rule of righteousness that whatever he wills, by the very fact that he wills it, must be considered righteous. When, therefore, one asks why God has so done, we must reply: because he has willed it. But if you proceed further to ask why he so willed, you are seeking something greater and higher than God's will, which cannot be found. Let men's rashness, then, restrain itself, and not seek what does not exist, lest perhaps it fail to find what does exist."[38] This attitude toward the sovereign will of God Calvin called a "bridle" that "will effectively restrain anyone who wants to ponder in reverence the secrets of his God."[39]

This constitutes Calvin's basic response to those who charge that God is unjust to hold us responsible for what He Himself has decreed. Calvin did, however, go on to indicate that God could "restrain his enemies" by "keeping silence."[40] Yet in His Word God has supplied us with weapons against these objectors. Scripture makes clear that the sovereign God owes nothing to human beings; He owes even less to those who are now all "vitiated by sin" so that

35. Ibid. (OS, 4:395f.).

36. Ibid.

37. Ibid. (OS, 4:396). Cf. the French *Institutes*, which speaks of "the reverie of the popish theologians."

38. Ibid.

39. Ibid.

40. Ibid., 3.23.3 (OS, 4:396).

we are all "odious to God." [41] Hence Calvin urged the objector to look at himself and recognize his sin; God is just in condemning the sinner even if the sinner cannot fathom the justice of God's eternal decree. To the objector who regards that answer as an evasion, "a subterfuge such as those who lack a just excuse are wont to have," Calvin suggested that we "ponder who God is." He asked: "For how could he who is the Judge of the earth allow any iniquity [cf. Gen. 18:25]?" [42] The apostle Paul was not looking for "loopholes of escape" when he indicated that "divine righteousness is higher than man's standard can measure, or than man's slender wit can comprehend." [43]

Calvin's answer to the charge that God is unjust emphasizes both the sovereignty and the justice of God's will. With Augustine he said: ". . . the Lord has created those whom he unquestionably foreknew would go to destruction. This has happened because he has so willed it. But why he so willed it is not for our reason to inquire, for we cannot comprehend it. And it is not fitting that God's will should be dragged down into controversy among us, for whenever mention is made of it, under its name is designated the supreme rule of righteousness." [44] Since God's justice is clearly evident in His final condemnation of the unbelieving sinner, who deserves nothing less than condemnation, "why raise any question of unrighteousness where righteousness clearly appears?" [45]

Calvin's firm insistence upon the sovereignty of God's will in reprobation leads the objector to suggest that God must then have willed man's sin. Opponents suggested that Calvin's doctrine of reprobation frees the sinner from responsibility and actually makes God the author of sin. Calvin also considered this objection. He readily admitted that God had willed Adam's fall,[46] but he denied that God is the author of sin or that God's decree removes the sinner's responsibility.

---

41. Ibid.
42. Ibid., 3.23.4 (OS, 4:398).
43. Ibid.
44. Ibid., 3.23.5 (OS, 4:398).
45. Ibid.
46. See chapter 2, note 15 on the infralapsarian-supralapsarian question. Calvin cited no specific passage for his view, but see *Institutes* 3.23.7, 8.

With respect to God's willing the fall, Calvin stated:

> Scripture proclaims that all mortals were bound over to eternal death in the person of one man [cf. Rom. 5:12ff.]. Since this cannot be ascribed to nature, it is perfectly clear that it has come forth from the wonderful plan of God. . . . The decree is dreadful (*decretum horribile*) indeed, I confess. Yet no one can deny that God foreknew what end man was to have before he created him, and consequently foreknew because he so ordained by his decree. . . . And it ought not to seem absurd for me to say that God not only foresaw the fall of the first man, and in him the ruin of his descendants, but also meted it out in accordance with his own decision. For as it pertains to his wisdom to foreknow everything that is to happen, so it pertains to his might to rule and control everything by his hand.[47]

Not only Adam's fall, but also that of all his posterity is included in God's will.

> Of course, I admit that in this miserable condition wherein men are now bound, all of Adam's children have fallen by God's will. And this is what I said to begin with, that we must always at last return to the sole decision of God's will, the cause of which is hidden in him.[48]

Calvin acknowledged, then, that God had willed Adam's fall. Yet Calvin did not fully understand or comprehend this: "For the first man fell because the Lord had judged it to be expedient; why he so judged is hidden from us."[49] Calvin did add, ". . . it is certain that he so judged because he saw that thereby the glory of his name is duly revealed."[50] Beyond that recognition Calvin did not go. The evident cause of condemnation, he again asserted, is "the corrupt nature of humanity," but the "hidden and utterly incomprehensible cause"[51] lies in God's predestination. Hence Calvin

---

47. Ibid., 3.23.7 (OS, 4:401f.).

48. Ibid., 3.23.4 (OS, 4:397).

49. Ibid., 3.23.8 (OS, 4:402).

50. Ibid.

51. Ibid.

concluded: "And let us not be ashamed to submit our understanding to God's boundless wisdom so far as to yield before its many secrets. For, of those things which it is neither given nor lawful to know, ignorance is learned; the craving to know, a kind of madness."[52]

In connection with Adam's fall and God's decree, some of Calvin's opponents distinguished between God's will and His permission. "By this they would maintain that the wicked perish because God permits it, not because he so wills."[53] Calvin rejected that distinction. (The reference here to *permission* must not be confused with the term *permissive decree* employed by some Reformed theologians. The permissive decree concerns God's decree and His will. Calvin was contemplating a distinction between *will* and *permission*.) He acknowledged of course that when men sin, "the whole fault rests with themselves. . . . But to turn all those passages of Scripture (wherein the affection of the mind, in the act, is distinctly described) into a mere permission on the part of God is a frivolous subterfuge, and a vain attempt to escape from the mighty truth!"[54] Some of the church fathers—even Augustine at first— were too eager to avoid giving offense; but by using the term *permission* they "relaxed something of that fixedness of attention which was due to the great truth itself."[55] Calvin contended that those passages that speak of God's blinding and hardening the reprobate, as well as the references to Joseph, Job, David, and Paul, show that the term *permission* is inadequate. The sinner is always responsible for his sin, but even these sins are somehow included in the incomprehensible will of God, who does not simply permit but "rules and overrules all the actions of the world with perfect and divine rectitude."[56] In other words, "man falls according as God's providence ordains, but he falls by his own fault."[57]

---

52. Ibid.

53. Ibid.

54. *Brief Reply*, in *Theological Treatises*, p. 201 (OC, 9:263).

55. Ibid.

56. Ibid., p. 203 (OC, 9:264).

57. *Institutes* 3.23.8 (OS, 4:402ff.). "*Cadit igitur homo, Dei providentia sic ordinante: sed suo vitio cadit.*"

Calvin's insistence upon God's will as the cause of the decree of reprobation and his objection to the term *permission* with respect to human sin led his opponents to charge that this view makes God the author of sin. Calvin considered this "an atrocious charge."[58] He called upon his opponents to be cautious in the words they used and the charges they made; such unwarranted charges could lead simple and inexperienced Christians to "dash against the awful and abhorrent rock of making God the author of sin."[59] Calvin admitted that no words of his can unravel this mystery. But, convinced that Scripture teaches that God's will is the ultimate cause of all things, he was willing to leave the mystery there.

One senses the disgust with which Calvin heard the critics' demand for explanation. "As if it were mine to render an exact reason for the secret counsels of God," he wrote rhetorically, "and to make mortals understand, to a pin's point that heavenly wisdom, the height and depth of which they are commanded to look upon and adore."[60] In another place he suggested that those troubled by this problem should take Augustine's advice: "You, a man, expect an answer from me; I too am a man. Therefore, let both of us hear one who says, 'O man, who are you?' [Rom. 9:20]. Ignorance that believes is better than rash knowledge. . . . Paul rested, for he found wonder. He calls God's judgments 'unsearchable,' and thou settest out to search them? He speaks of his ways as 'inscrutable' [Rom. 11:33], and thou dost track them down?"[61] Following that advice himself, Calvin simply added that "it will do us no good to proceed farther. . . ."[62]

Where Calvin did discuss these questions in greater detail, he only enlarged the same response and introduced certain distinctions. For example, Calvin suggested that if the view that God had decreed Adam's fall makes God the author of sin, then one is also forced to say that God is the author of that wicked act by which

---

58. *Brief Reply*, in *Theological Treatises*, p. 190 (OC, 9:258). See also the letter to the syndics of Geneva (1552), in *Letters*, 2:348–54.

59. *Brief Reply*, in *Theological Treatises*, p. 191 (OC, 9:258).

60. Ibid., p. 194 (OC, 9:260).

61. *Institutes* 3.23.5 (OS, 4:399).

62. Ibid.

the Jews crucified Jesus Christ. The Jews did "that which Thy hand
and Thy counsel beforehand determined to be done"; and remember, said Calvin, that these "are not the words of Calvin, but
of the Holy Spirit and of Peter, and of the whole primitive
church." [63]

A distinction Calvin considered helpful here is that between the
will of God and the will of Satan: "There is . . . a mighty difference, because although God and the devil will the same thing,
they do so in an utterly different manner . . . man will[s] with
an evil will that which God wills with a good will." [64] Calvin insisted that "God is, and must be, ever utterly remote from sin." [65]
As Augustine ably expressed it: "By an inexplicable manner of
operation, that is not done without the will of God which is, in
itself, even contrary to His will, because without His will it could
not have been done at all. And yet God willeth not unwillingly,
but willingly." [66] The godly man, according to Calvin, will "indeed
confess that the fall of Adam was not without the rule and overrule
of the secret providence of God (*arcana Dei providentia*), but they
never doubt that the end and object of his secret counsel were
righteous and just. But as the reason lies hidden in the mind of
God, they soberly and reverently await the revelation of it, which
shall be made in the day in which we shall see that God 'face to
face,' whom we now 'behold through a glass darkly' and unin-
telligently." [67]

Another distinction that Calvin thought helpful in considering
this question is that between ultimate and proximate causes. In
Calvin's judgment this very simple distinction is of great importance. Calvin was not surprised that his opponent Pighius "should
indiscriminately confuse everything in the judgments of God, when

---

63. *Brief Reply*, in *Theological Treatises*, p. 191 (OC, 9:258).

64. Ibid., p. 196 (OC, 9:261). Calvin was quoting Augustine in the
latter part.

65. Ibid., p. 195 (OC, 9:261).

66. Ibid., p. 200 (OC, 9:263).

67. Ibid., p. 197 (OC, 9:261).

he does not distinguish between causes proximate and remote." [68]
Calvin considered it "wicked and calumnious" of Pighius to charge
that Calvin made the fall of man "one of the works of God" since
Calvin, "removing from God all proximate causation of the act . . .
at the same time remove[s] from Him all guilt and leave[s] man
alone liable." [69] Yet this helpful distinction did not solve the mystery
for Calvin: ". . . but how it was ordained by the foreknowledge
and decree of God what man's future was without God being impli-
cated as associate in the fault as the author or approver of trans-
gression, is clearly a secret so much excelling the insight of the
human mind, that I am not ashamed to confess ignorance." [70]

For Calvin, then, God's sovereign will is the ultimate cause of
Adam's fall and of reprobation, while human sin is the proximate
cause. In the latter—in man's sin—lies all the blame and guilt. In
seeking to understand these difficult questions, Calvin therefore
urged that we emphasize what is clear and understandable—man's
personal guilt—and not unduly scrutinize what Scripture also
teaches clearly—God's will as the ultimate cause—but which we
cannot comprehend. The clear explanation of the unbeliever's condemnation is his own guilt; that is Calvin's repeated emphasis. "By
his own evil intention, then, man corrupted the pure nature he had
received from the Lord; and by his fall he drew all his posterity
with him into destruction. Accordingly, we should contemplate the
evident cause of condemnation in the corrupt nature of humanity—
which is closer to us—rather than seek a hidden and utterly incomprehensible cause in God's predestination." [71] This is where
"ignorance is learned" and "the craving to know, a kind of madness." [72] Calvin followed his own advice, as this rare personal con-

---

68. *Eternal Predestination*, p. 100 (OC, 8:296). Cf. Calvin's comments
on Rom. 9:11 in *Romans* (OC, 49:177–79) and in the letter to ministers
of Switzerland (1551) in *Letters*, 2:310. Notice that T. F. Torrance,
among others, failed to make this distinction between proximate and ultimate causes and hence failed to reproduce Calvin's thought accurately at
this point. *Calvin's Doctrine of Man*, p. 106. See also note 96 below.

69. *Eternal Predestination*, pp. 123–28 (OC, 8:316).

70. Ibid., p. 124.

71. *Institutes* 3.23.8 (OS, 4:403).

72. Ibid.

fession indicates: "I prescribe nothing to others but what comes out of the experience of my heart. For the Lord is my witness, and my conscience attests it, that I daily so meditate on these mysteries of His judgments that curiosity to know anything more does not attract me; no sinister suspicion concerning His justice steals away my confidence; no desire to complain entices me."[73]

Reprobation and election are equally ultimate. Calvin's distinction between ultimate and proximate causes provides a good context in which to examine the question of the equal ultimacy of election and reprobation. While Calvin's opponents always objected to the entire doctrine of reprobation, some of his friends today contend that he did not regard election and reprobation as equally ultimate. What does this assertion mean? The discussions have generally failed, unfortunately, to indicate clearly what it does mean.[74]

This question has a clear focus if we refer to Calvin's distinction between ultimate and proximate causes. If the term "equal ultimacy" refers to the ultimate cause of election and reprobation, the question is not difficult to answer from Calvin's writings. Is the sovereign will of God, according to Calvin, the ultimate cause of reprobation as it is of election? The various statements of Calvin, cited in the discussion above, provide a clear affirmative answer to this question. Calvin affirmed that the will of God, His eternal decree, is the ultimate cause of reprobation as well as of election. Human sin and guilt enter significantly into Calvin's discussion of reprobation, of course, but this sin and guilt constitute the proximate cause, not of reprobation as such, but of the judicial element of reprobation, namely, eternal condemnation. Calvin urged his readers

---

73. *Eternal Predestination*, p. 124 (OC, 8:316).

74. Cf. Edward A. Dowey, Jr., *The Knowledge of God in Calvin's Theology*, pp. 211f.; Torrance, *Kingdom and Church*, p. 107; Heinrich Quistorp, *Calvin's Doctrine of the Last Things*, pp. 144ff.; Paul Van Buren, *Christ in Our Place: The Substitutionary Character of Calvin's Doctrine of Reconciliation*, pp. 102f.; Cornelius Van Til, *The Defense of the Faith*, pp. 413ff.; Van Til, *The Theology of James Daane*, pp. 59–79; James Daane, *A Theology of Grace*, pp. 13–144; Daane, *The Freedom of God: A Study of Election and Pulpit*, pp. 165ff.; Daane, "The Principle of Equal Ultimacy of Election and Reprobation."

to look at this proximate or "evident cause of condemnation"[75] because they could readily recognize and understand this; God's justice is apparent in His condemnation of the guilty unbeliever. But Calvin never allowed this reference to the proximate cause of reprobation [condemnation] to stand by itself. Compelled by the teaching of Scripture, he acknowledged that the ultimate or remote cause of reprobation, as of election, is the sovereign will of God. However incomprehensible this is, Calvin submitted to the teaching of Scripture.

Although the reader will find sufficient evidence for Calvin's view of equal ultimacy in the summary of his views above,[76] the importance of the subject in recent debates warrants a brief summary of the evidence here. The opening section of Calvin's discussion of predestination is already entitled "Eternal Election, by which God has Predestined Some to Salvation, Others to Destruction."[77] His basic definition of predestination has the same force:

> As Scripture, then, clearly shows, we say that God once established by his eternal and unchangeable plan those whom he long before determined once for all to receive into salvation, and those whom, on the other hand, he would devote to destruction. We assert that, with respect to the elect, this plan was founded upon his freely given mercy, without regard to human worth; but by his just and irreprehensible but incomprehensible judgment he has barred the door of life to those whom he has given over to damnation.[78]

He defined predestination as "God's eternal decree, by which he compacted with himself what he willed to become of each man. . . . Eternal life is foreordained for some, eternal damnation for others."[79] One is "predestined to life or to death."[80] "By his secret

---

75. *Institutes* 3.23.8 (OS. 4:403). See quotation in note 71 above.

76. Compare the headings of the first two main sections of chapter 2 with those of chapter 3.

77. *Institutes* 3.21 (OS, 4:368).

78. Ibid., 3.21.7 (OS, 4:368).

79. Ibid., 3.21.5 (OS, 4:374). Cf. Dowey, *Knowledge of God*, pp. 211–12. Dowey admitted that there is "apparent equality" in this statement of

plan" God "freely chooses whom he pleases, rejecting others." [81]
After discussing the Biblical basis for election and reprobation,
Calvin concluded: "Do you see how Paul attributes both to God's
decision alone? If, then, we cannot determine a reason why he
vouchsafes mercy to his own, except that it so pleases him, neither
shall we have any reason for rejecting others, other than his will.
For when it is said that God hardens or shows mercy to whom he
wills, men are warned by this to seek no cause outside his will." [82]

As he refuted "the false accusations with which this doctrine has
always been unjustly burdened," [83] Calvin again clearly linked
reprobation ultimately to the will of God. He stated that "those
whom God passes over (*praeterit*), he condemns (*reprobat*); and
this he does for no other reason than that he wills to exclude them
from the inheritance which he predestines for his own children." [84]
After citing key references in Romans 9, Calvin urged his readers
to "note that Paul, to cut off occasion for whispering and disparagement, gives the ultimate sovereignty to God's wrath and might,"
and he added that "God's secret plan is the cause of hardening." [85]
In considering the relation of Adam's fall to God's decree, Calvin
said, "Of course, I admit that in this miserable condition wherein
men are now bound, all of Adam's children have fallen by God's
will." [86] He continued, "And this is what I said to begin with, that
we must always at last return to the sole decision of God's will,
the cause of which is hidden in him." [87] Not only election and salvation but also reprobation and condemnation find their ultimate
cause in the sovereign will of God. "Since the disposition of all

Calvin, but then he attempted to show, on epistemological and logical
grounds, that the "element of reprobation is subordinate to that of election." Pp. 212–19.

80. *Institutes* 3.21.5 (OS, 4:374).

81. Ibid., 3.21.7 (OS, 4:377).

82. Ibid., 3.22.11 (OS, 4:393).

83. Calvin's title for 3.23.

84. Ibid., 3.23.1 (OS, 4:394).

85. Ibid. (OS, 4:394–95).

86. Ibid., 3.23.4 (OS, 4:397).

87. Ibid.

things is in God's hand, since the decision of salvation or of death rests in his power, he so ordains by his plan and will. . . ." [88] God's foreknowledge rests on "the fact that he decreed that they take place," and "it is clear that all things take place . . . by his determination and bidding." [89]

When Calvin spoke of the means by which God executes His decree, he again referred the ultimate cause of reprobation to the sovereign will of God: "For all are not created in equal condition; rather, eternal life is foreordained for some, eternal damnation for others." [90] With Augustine, Calvin said: "The Lord has created those whom he unquestionably foreknew would go to destruction. This has happened because he has so willed it. But why he so willed, it is not for our reason to inquire, for we cannot comprehend it." [91] When one asks why the gospel is preached to some nations and not to others, and why some to whom it is preached believe and others do not, "he who here seeks a deeper cause (*causam altiorem*) than God's secret and inscrutable plan will torment himself to no purpose." [92] Yet Calvin was always concerned to add that "none undeservedly perish." [93] And when his discussion centered on human responsibility, the addition concerned God's sovereignty, as this statement illustrates: "The fact that the reprobate do not obey God's Word when it is made known to them will be justly charged against the malice and depravity of their hearts, provided it is added at the same time that they have been raised up by the just but inscrutable judgment of God to show forth his glory in their condemnation." [94]

This summary clearly indicates that Calvin regarded the ultimate cause of reprobation, as well as election, as the sovereign will of God. The number of quotations could easily be multiplied from

---

88. Ibid., 3.23.6 (OS, 4:401). See chap. 2, note 18 above.

89. Ibid.

90. Ibid., 3.21.5 (OS, 4:374). Cf. 3.23.5.

91. Ibid., 3.23.5 (OS, 4:398).

92. Ibid., 3.24.12 (OS, 4:423).

93. Ibid. (OS, 4:424).

94. Ibid., 3.24.14 (OS, 4:426).

Calvin's other writings.[95] His contemporary opponents understood him correctly on this score: Calvin clearly regarded the sovereign will of God as the ultimate cause of reprobation as well as of election. If the term *"equal ultimacy"* refers to the ultimate cause of election and reprobation, Calvin clearly taught the equal ultimacy of election and reprobation. In answering the false accusations made against the doctrine of predestination, Calvin never retreated from his emphatic insistence that the will of God is the ultimate cause of reprobation.[96]

Reprobation and election are not completely parallel. If election and reprobation are *equally* ultimate in the sense that the sovereign will of God is the ultimate cause of each, this does *not* mean that, for Calvin, election and reprobation are *in all aspects parallel.* Recent discussions of the question have, unfortunately, not distinguished these two facets of the subject. The result has been confusion, distortion, and bypassing of other scholars' arguments. When ultimacy and parallelism are not clearly defined and distinguished, a simple denial of equal ultimacy usually involves a distortion of Calvin's insistence upon the sovereignty of the divine will in reprobation.[97] While insisting on Calvin's defense of the equal ultimacy of election and reprobation, however, we must also do justice to the ways in which Calvin indicated they are not parallel.

The nonparallel features of election and reprobation stand out in the chapter titles of this book. While both election and reprobation are described as "sovereign" (indicating the equal ultimacy of the two in Calvin's theology), election is further described as "gratuitous," reprobation as "just."

One of the most striking indications of the lack of parallelism is evident in Calvin's insistence on distinguishing the ultimate and proximate causes of reprobation. Human sinful action is the proximate cause of the condemnation aspect of reprobation. But Calvin

---

95. E.g., see *Eternal Predestination*, pp. 68f., 76ff., 155ff. (OC, 8:296ff.).

96. *Institutes* 3.21; *Eternal Predestination*, p. 100.

97. This is the point Van Til is eager to defend in insisting on the equal ultimacy of election and reprobation. *The Defense of the Faith*, p. 415.

never referred to human action as being even a proximate cause of divine election. In fact the ground of election is Jesus Christ, and it is precisely our election in Christ that indicates that nothing in human persons is even a proximate cause of election. With regard to reprobation, however, sinful human actions do come into consideration. It is crucial to note at just what point Calvin considered these as the proximate cause of reprobation. We have seen indications of Calvin's distinction between *preterition* ("passing by") and *condemnation.* Although later Reformed theologians used these terms technically, the distinction had been made by Calvin as well. Sinful human action was not regarded by Calvin as the proximate cause of God's sovereign passing by of some while electing others. This decision he credited solely to the freedom of God, to His sovereign will and free decision. It is not because of sinful actions that God decrees to pass some by with His grace. Works, neither performed nor forseen, play no role at this point in Calvin's thought. If sinful works were the proximate cause of the preterition aspect of reprobation, there would be no election.

Sinful actions are the proximate cause only of the condemnation aspect of reprobation. While God sovereignly passes some by in His decretive will, the ground of His final condemnation of them is their sin and guilt. This sin is our sin; it constitutes the proximate cause of reprobation as far as the unbeliever's condemnation is concerned. It is important to observe, however, that sin is not the ground or the proximate cause of God's ultimate discrimination between elect and reprobate. We have heard Calvin deny that often enough.[98] But condemnation, while sovereignly executed, is always the result of human sin—". . . none undeservedly perish."[99] Sin and guilt are the basis for the judicial sentence of condemnation.[100] Calvin's reference to the proximate cause of condemnation in reprobation is one respect in which election and reprobation are not parallel.

---

98. See chap. 2, notes 22–26 above.

99. *Institutes* 3.24.12 (OS, 4:424).

100. This emphasis of Calvin is very accurately reflected in the Westminster Confession, 3.8. Cf. John Murray, "The Theology of the Westminster Standards," pp. 113f.; and *Calvin on Scripture and Divine Sovereignty*, pp. 55–71.

Another nonparallel aspect of election and reprobation is closely linked to the preceding one; indeed it is involved in it. We have seen that according to Calvin, Christ is the ground of God's decree of election.[101] The objects of God's eternal election were unworthy of the grace that He chose to give them; God looked upon them in Christ.[102] Christ was the Head in whom the Father united all His elect. In Calvin's doctrine of reprobation, there is no parallel to this key feature of election. The reprobate are obviously not reprobate in Christ. Nor does Calvin see Satan as their head; the reprobate are not reprobate in Satan. In his commentary on Matthew, Calvin did assert that the devil is the head of all the reprobate and the adversary of Christ,[103] but he did not bring this perspective into the discussion of the *decree* of reprobation. Calvin did observe that in many parts of Scripture, the devil is represented as the head of the fallen angels and as the one who gathers all the impious together into one mass of corruption.[104] But Calvin did not refer to this in his discussion of reprobation and the eternal decree. Hence, in explaining Calvin's doctrine of reprobation, we cannot say that he set forth a ground of reprobation in Satan.

It would also be improper to say that the ground of reprobation is man's sin and guilt.[105] Sin and guilt may be said to be the ground of only one element of reprobation, namely, condemnation; sin is the proximate cause of reprobation only in this sense. Even then, however, it is only the proximate cause. As proximate cause, it is clearly understood by us while the ultimate cause is not. On this proximate cause Calvin did place great emphasis, and concentration upon it makes crystal clear that God is just; the blame for sin and final condemnation is ours, not God's.

There are other respects in which election and reprobation are

---

101. See chap. 2, notes 95ff. above.

102. See chap. 2, notes 53–58 above.

103. Cf. Calvin's comments on Matt. 24:41 in OC, 73:690.

104. Ibid.

105. *Eternal Predestination*, pp. 120–21 (OC, 8:313). "When God prefers some to others, choosing some and passing others by, the difference does not depend on human dignity or indignity. It is therefore wrong to say that the reprobate are worthy of eternal destruction." Hence this section of our summary cannot be called the "ground" of reprobation.

not parallel. Sometimes it is said that Calvin gave less space or attention to reprobation than to election. That contention is difficult to maintain, however, since reprobation is constantly involved in Calvin's discussion of election. Besides, he certainly defended the doctrine of reprobation against all sorts of attack and opposition, from friend as well as foe. Yet it is obviously true that Calvin did not show the same interest and delight in sovereign, just reprobation that he did in sovereign, gratuitous election. He certainly had no interest in reprobation that reflects personal desire or national or schizoid characteristics.[106] He taught the doctrine and defended it vigorously because he was convinced that Scripture teaches it. He was confident that what the Holy Spirit had revealed in Scripture has a purpose that may not be despised or ignored. In his attempted fidelity to the written Word of God, he was confident that he was being submissive to the sovereign God and obedient to Jesus Christ. In all of this, his sole aim was the glory of God.

This Biblical source led Calvin to delight in God's election and to stress it in his preaching in a way that is not possible with respect to reprobation. We have already noted that Calvin considered it a serious error to minimize human responsibility with respect to the Word preached. An unbiblical view of reprobation would also be irresponsible.[107] When an opponent charged that according to Calvin "God had by his pure and mere will created the greatest part of the world to perdition," Calvin replied that this was "a perfect fiction" produced in the workshop of the opponent's brain: "For although God did certainly decree from the beginning everything which should befall the race of man, yet such a manner of speech as the saying that the end or object of God's work of creation was destruction or perdition, is nowhere to be found in my writings. . . . God never decrees anything but with the most righteous reason."[108]

Having noted various nonparallel features of election and repro-

---

106. Cf. Herman Bauke, *Die Probleme der Theologie Calvins*, p. 14; Hermann Weber, *Die Theologie Calvins: Ihre inner Systematik im Lichte structurpsychologiescher Forschungsmethode*, pp. 18, 24f.

107. See chap. 2, note 72 above.

108. *Secret Providence of God*, in *Theological Treatises*, pp. 266f. (OC, 9:288). See also his denial that God is "absolute, or tyrannical will," as some scholastics maintained that He is.

bation, we must finally observe those features that *are* parallel. The most striking one is that God's sovereign will is the ultimate cause of each. In that respect we have spoken of the equal ultimacy of election and reprobation.[109] There is a parallel also in the fact that the works of human persons are the cause of neither the decree of election nor the decree of reprobation. Election and reprobation are also parallel in that each in its own way contributes to the ultimate glory of God. Another parallel is the fact that God decrees not only the end and goal, but also the means to the attainment of each decreed goal. We must still consider the means of reprobation in the following section; there it will become clear that although there is a parallel, reprobation is effected in the "reverse way" from election.

Although other features could be mentioned as parallel or non-parallel, two issues stand out in Calvin's discussion. God is sovereign in reprobation as well as in election; they are equally ultimate. But it is God's justice or righteousness that stands out in reprobation, while the free, gratuitous mercy of God characterizes election. When the reprobate finally receive the eternal punishment that awaits them, they receive precisely what they deserve. But when the elect receive the eternal salvation that awaits them, they receive what they do *not* deserve. The elect receive graciously, though also justly, the continued favor and undeserved mercy of God through Jesus Christ. This is the chief respect in which election and reprobation are not parallel—though they are equally ultimate.

The Goal and Means of Reprobation

The goal is God's glory. In Calvin's thought the goal or final cause of election is the praise and glory of God; the goal of reprobation is the glory of God also. Indeed, everything God does manifests His glory: ". . . the whole world is constituted for the end of being a theatre of His glory."[110] Romans 9 indicates that even reprobation has the glory of God as its goal, for there Paul said "that the repro-

---

109. See notes 74–97 above. Also Gerrit C. Berkouwer failed to do justice to this emphasis of Calvin. *Divine Election*, especially chap. 6, "Election and Rejection," pp. 172–217.

110. *Eternal Predestination*, p. 97 (OC, 8:294). Cf. *Institutes* 1.3–5.

bate are raised up to the end that through them God's glory may be revealed."[111] Scripture indicates "that the wicked were created for the day of evil simply because God willed to illustrate His own glory in them [Prov. 16:4]; just as elsewhere He declares that Pharaoh was raised up by Him that He might show forth His name among the Gentiles (Exod. 9:16)."[112]

In Calvin's judgment the glory of God includes His justice. He illustrates this with respect to the fall. Man is responsible for his sin, yet Adam's fall was predestined by God (although the human mind cannot understand why God willed it). "Yet it is certain that he [God] so judged because he saw that thereby the glory of his name is duly revealed."[113] Calvin immediately continued: "Where you hear God's glory mentioned, think of his justice. For whatever deserves praise must be just."[114] Even in the destruction of the wicked, then, the glory of God is manifest. Again in reference to Proverbs 16:4, Calvin wrote: "Behold! Since the disposition of all things is in God's hand, since the decision of salvation or of death rests in his power, he so ordains by his plan and will that among men some are born destined for certain death from the womb, who glorify his name by their own destruction."[115]

Three complex factors work together in contributing to God's glory: the eternal decree of God, the wickedness of man, and the final condemnation of the unbeliever by a just God. Calvin intertwined these three factors in this way: "The fact that the reprobate do not obey God's Word when it is made known to them will be justly charged against the malice and depravity of their hearts, provided it be added at the same time that they have been raised up by the just but inscrutable judgment of God to show forth his glory in their condemnation."[116] As one might expect, the complex interrelationship of these three factors led Calvin once again to acknowledge the mystery and incomprehensibility of it all. While Scripture

---

111. *Institutes* 3.22.11 (OS, 4:393).

112. *Eternal Predestination*, p. 97 (OC, 8:293).

113. *Institutes* 3.23.8 (OS, 4:402).

114. Ibid.

115. Ibid., 3.23.6 (OS, 4:400).

116. Ibid., 3.24.14 (OS, 4:426).

clearly teaches it, godly minds cannot "reconcile the two matters, that man when first made was set in such a position that by voluntarily falling he should be the cause of his own destruction, and yet that it was so ordained by the admirable counsel of God that this voluntary ruin to the human race and all the posterity of Adam should be a cause of humility."[117] Scripture reveals that "the Lord has made everything for its purpose, even the wicked for the day of trouble" (Prov. 16:4 RSV). Whether man can comprehend it or not, he must believe and accept it. Hence Calvin insisted that the eternal decree of reprobation has the glory of God for its final goal.

The means are diverse. Calvin understood the decree of God to include the means for bringing about the decree's goal or purpose. We have seen this in connection with the decree of election: those whom God elected, He also calls, justifies, and glorifies (Rom. 8:29–30). While Calvin taught that the decree of reprobation includes the means for bringing about the decreed goal, he also introduced some important qualifications. God is certainly not the author of sin; the very idea is blasphemous in Calvin's judgment. God hates sin; He never commands anyone to sin. Rather, He commands always, "Thou shalt not . . ." Furthermore, as we have seen repeatedly, Calvin always insisted that human beings are responsible for their sin. Because God's decree always includes the means for its effectuation, there is a parallel here between decree and means with respect to both election and reprobation. Yet the relation of decree and means in reprobation is the "reverse" of what it is in election.[118] That is to say, God withholds from the reprobate what He gives to the elect. He enlightens the hearts of the elect by His Spirit while He abandons the reprobate and withholds His grace

---

117. *Eternal Predestination*, p. 98 (OC, 8:294f.). Compare Calvin's comments on Romans 9:22, where the glory of God manifested in the destruction of the reprobate is said to occur "so that this may make the extent of His mercy toward the elect better known and shine with greater clarity. . . ." In commenting on Romans 9:23, Calvin interpreted "the word *glory*, which is twice repeated here, to mean, by metonymy, the mercy of God. God's chief praise consists in acts of kindness."

118. Cf. *Thessalonians* (on II Thess. 2:11). OC, 52:204. In election God grants, softens, and enlightens; in reprobation He withholds, hardens, and blinds.

from them, blinding them in their sin, hardening their hearts, and handing them over to Satan.[119] "But as the Lord seals his elect by call and justification," Calvin wrote in the *Institutes*, "so, by shutting off the reprobate from knowledge of his name or from the sanctification of his Spirit, he, as it were, reveals by these marks what sort of judgment awaits them."[120]

In another context Calvin expressed even more fully this relation of the decree and the means of achieving the decree's goal:

> As God by the effectual working of his call to the elect perfects the salvation to which by his eternal plan he has destined them, so he has his judgments against the reprobate, by which he executes his plan for them. What of those, then, whom he created for dishonor in life and destruction in death, to become the instruments of his wrath and examples of his severity? That they may come to their end, he sometimes deprives them of the capacity to hear his word; at other times he, rather, blinds and stuns them by the preaching of it. . . . The supreme Judge, then, makes way for his predestination when he leaves in blindness those whom he has once condemned and deprived of participation in his light.[121]

As this quotation indicates, Calvin recognized diversity in the means God uses to execute His plan of reprobation. Some people may be deprived of the privilege of hearing the gospel. The clearest example is the period from Babel to Pentecost, when divine revelation was largely confined to the chosen nation of Israel and withheld from the Gentiles. Why were Gentile nations deprived of hearing the Word of God? "He who here seeks a deeper cause than God's secret and inscrutable plan will torment himself to no purpose," is Calvin's answer.[122]

---

119. Ibid. Cf. also comments on Rom. 9.

120. 3.21.7 (OS, 4:379). "*Quemadmodum.* . . ."

121. Ibid., 3.24.12 (OS, 4:423). "*Quemadmodum.* . . ."

122. Ibid. (OS, 4:424). In order to understand Calvin's argument here and his insistence upon the justice of God, who withholds His Word from some, it must be remembered that Calvin believed that all people are continuously confronted with God's general revelation, but that they suppress this revelation in their sinful unbelief. Cf. 1.3–5 and Ps. 19 and Rom. 1:18ff.

The means God employs to execute His decree sometimes take a different, more dramatic form. "That the Lord sends his Word to many whose blindness he intends to increase cannot indeed be called in question."[123] Pharaoh is a striking example, as Paul showed in Romans 9. "For what purpose does he [God] cause so many demands to be made upon Pharaoh? Is it because he hoped to soften his heart by oft-repeated embassies? No, before he began, he both had known and had foretold the outcome."[124] Illustrations from Ezekiel, Jeremiah, and Isaiah show that "he directs his voice to them but in order that they may become even more blind; he sets forth doctrine but so that they may grow even more stupid; he employs a remedy but so that they may not be healed."[125] Jesus indicated that His parables had a similar purpose (Matt. 13:11); hence Calvin contended that "we cannot gainsay the fact that, to those whom he pleases not to illumine, God transmits his doctrine wrapped in enigmas in order that they may not profit by it except to be cast into greater stupidity."[126] The apostle John, referring to the prophecy of Isaiah, "states that the Jews could not believe Christ's teaching [John 12:39], for this curse of God hung over them."[127]

Man is still responsible. God's sovereign use of these various means to execute his decree of reprobation does not, however, eliminate or reduce human responsibility. In such contexts Calvin also emphasized human accountability; man is never excused for his unbelief. Jesus told His disciples that He spoke to the people in parables because "the knowledge of the secrets of the kingdom of heaven has been given to you, but not to them. . . . Though seeing, they do not see; though hearing, they do not understand" (Matt. 13:11, 13 NIV). "What does the Lord mean," Calvin asked, "by teaching those by whom he takes care not to be understood?"[128]

---

123. *Institutes* 3.24.13 (OS, 4:424f.).

124. Ibid. (OS, 4:425).

125. Ibid. Torrance gave to Calvin's use of the term *accidental* a meaning that conflicts with Calvin's clear assertions here. *Kingdom and Church*, p. 106.

126. *Institutes* 3.24.13 (OS, 4:425).

127. Ibid. Cf. *Eternal Predestination*, p. 94 (OC, 8:291).

128. *Institutes* 3.24.13 (OS, 4:425).

Here Calvin's answer emphasizes human unbelief: "Consider whose fault it is, and stop questioning. For however much obscurity there may be in the Word, there is still always enough light to convict the conscience of the wicked."[129] Here again human responsibility and divine sovereignty are incomprehensibly intertwined. Those who were "ordained to eternal life" hear and obey through the sovereign instrumentality of the Holy Spirit. Calvin also asked, "Why, then, does he bestow grace upon these but pass over others?"[130] The former, as Luke explained, "were appointed [ordained] for eternal life" (Acts 13:48); the latter, as Paul explained, were "the objects of his wrath—prepared for destruction" (Rom. 9:22).[131] In that light Calvin suggested that we "not be ashamed to say with Augustine: 'God could . . . turn the will of evil men to good because he is almighty. Obviously he could. Why, then, does he not? Because he wills otherwise. Why he wills otherwise rests with him.' "[132]

We have seen that Calvin recognized variety in the means God employs to execute His sovereign decree of reprobation. He withholds His Word from some; to others He sends His Word and through it blinds or hardens them in unbelief. Of course human irresponsibility is intertwined with the sovereign action of God. Yet Calvin always regarded the preaching of the gospel as evidence of the goodness of God. "When he first shines with the light of his Word upon the undeserving," Calvin maintained, "he thereby shows a sufficiently clear proof of his free goodness (*gratuitae bonitatis*)."[133] He continued: "Here, then, God's boundless goodness (*immensa Dei bonitas*) is already manifesting itself but not to the salvation of all; for a heavier judgment remains upon the wicked because they reject the testimony of God's love (*testimonium amoris Dei*)."[134] Although the Word is evidence of the free and

---

129. Ibid.

130. Ibid. (OS, 4:424).

131. Ibid.

132. Ibid.

133. Ibid., 3.24.2 (OS, 4:412). Cf. Herman Kuiper, *Calvin on Common Grace.*

134. *Institutes* 3.24.2 (OS, 4:412).

boundless goodness of God, a testimony of His love, the difference in responses also involves the sovereign action of God: "And God also, to show forth his glory, withdraws the effectual working of his Spirit from them,"[135] that is, from the reprobate. But to His elect He grants the effectual agency of the Spirit so that they come to believe in Jesus Christ.

The preaching of the gospel actually "streams forth from the wellspring of election"[136] and has its primary aim in bringing the elect to faith in Christ. Yet the gospel must be preached to all people indiscriminately, for in this way God works His sovereign will. But why has God commanded that it be preached to all? Here is part of Calvin's answer: "It is that the consciences of the godly may rest more secure, when they understand there is no difference among sinners provided faith be present. On the other hand, the wicked cannot claim they lack a sanctuary to which they may hie themselves from the bondage of sin, inasmuch as they, out of their own ungratefulness, reject it when offered."[137] The question is even more pointed when we ask why the gospel is to be preached to the reprobate as well as the elect. Of course in history we do not know who are reprobate. But God's command requires the universal preaching of His gospel, and He knows who are elect and who reprobate. Calvin also addressed this question: "When he [God] addresses the same Word to the reprobate, though not to correct them, he makes it serve another use: today to press them with the witness of conscience, and in the Day of Judgment to render them the more inexcusable. . . . Paul points out that teaching is not useless among the reprobate, because it is to them 'a fragrance from death to death' [II Cor. 2:16], yet 'a sweet fragrance to God' [II Cor. 2:15]."[138] Thus Calvin recognized that the Word preached to the reprobate renders him subject to "a heavier judgment."[139] It is "the occasion for severer condemnation,"[140] rendering him in the final

---

135. Ibid.

136. Ibid., 3.24.1 (OS, 4:410). Cf. chap. 2, note 65 above.

137. Ibid., 3.24.17 (OS, 4:430).

138. Ibid., 2.5.7 (OS, 3:303).

139. Ibid., 3.24.2 (OS, 4:412).

140. Ibid., 3.24.8 (OS, 4:419). It is also "a savor of death."

judgment "the more inexcusable."[141] Hence the general call of the gospel also functions as a means in effectuating God's decree of reprobation. Yet Calvin insisted that "even though only his outward call renders inexcusable those who hear it and do not obey, still it is truly considered evidence of God's grace, by which he reconciles men to himself."[142]

In these diverse ways Calvin understood that God executes his sovereign decree of reprobation. Although God is the ultimate cause who sovereignly works His own good pleasure, the blame and guilt of sin resides in man, the proximate cause, for man sins willfully and is responsible for rejecting the goodness of God. God's decree is finally carried out when He condemns the unbeliever for his sin. There the justice of God shines forth clearly, a justice that is included within His glory. Hence "the reprobate are hateful to God, and with very good reason," Calvin insisted; "for, deprived of his Spirit, they can bring forth nothing but reason for cursing."[143] Thus Calvin always referred to the proximate cause of condemnation (reprobation)—human sin and guilt; but Scripture did not allow him to negate the ultimate cause of reprobation (preterition)—the sovereign will of God. His understanding of Scripture and his obedience to it as the trustworthy Word of God controlled his theology of predestination. With confident faith he trusted in the full reliability of the Word of God even though he acknowledged the inability of the human mind to grasp it all. So Calvin concluded his discussion of the controversial subject of predestination with these words: "Now when many notions are adduced on both sides, let this be our conclusion: to tremble with Paul at so deep a mystery; but, if froward tongues clamor, not to be ashamed of this exclamation of his: 'Who are you, O man, to argue with God?' [Rom. 9:20, paraphrase]. For as Augustine truly contends, they who measure divine justice by the standard of human justice are acting perversely."[144]

---

141. Ibid., 2.5.5 (OS, 3:303).

142. Ibid., 3.24.15 (OS, 4:428). Note Calvin's occasional reference to the temporary and nonspecial work of the Spirit on some of the reprobate. Cf. 3.24.8; *Eternal Predestination*, pp. 131f., 135ff.

143. *Institutes* 3.24.17 (OS, 4:431).

144. Ibid.

Conclusion

WE HAVE NOW SURVEYED the main features of Calvin's doctrine of double predestination—God's sovereign and gracious election and His sovereign and just reprobation. This doctrine in its totality has not been and probably never will be popular. We have seen that it is not personal preference but Scriptural teaching that compelled Calvin to believe, teach, and defend it. The unpopularity of this humbling doctrine is due in part, perhaps, to the fact that people do not readily submit to the full teaching of Scripture. We may observe, therefore, that one test of our fidelity to Scripture may be how Calvin's doctrine of predestination fares in the crisis of our age.

This was also Calvin's concern as he concluded his significant treatise *Concerning the Eternal Predestination of God*:

> I repeat what I said at the beginning. No one can disprove the doctrine I have expounded except he who pretends to be wiser than the Spirit of God. . . . For my part, I soberly and reverently confess that I know no other law of modesty than that which I learned in the school of the heavenly Master. But I am not unaware that prudence should be shown in tempering everything to the building up of faith. But as I have studied in good faith to do just this, even if the niceties of some are not yet satisfied, I fancy I have done my duty. He that has ears, let him hear.[1]

---

1. P. 161 (OC, 8:346f.).

This is the key to Calvin's doctrine of predestination. He listened to God as He spoke through His holy Word, the Scriptures. Calvin's doctrine of predestination is his attempt to faithfully echo what he heard the Scriptures say. His aim was to glorify God.

At the same time Calvin found out that obedience to the Word of God and thus the believing acceptance of this doctrine leads to the discovery of "the usefulness of this doctrine" and of "its very sweet fruit." Hence our summary of Calvin's teaching on this subject should end with his opening words:

> We shall never be clearly persuaded, as we ought to be, that our salvation flows from the wellspring of God's free mercy until we come to know his eternal election, which illumines God's grace by this contrast: that he does not indiscriminately adopt all into the hope of salvation but gives to some what he denies to others.
>
> How much the ignorance of this principle detracts from God's glory, how much it takes away from true humility, is well known. . . . If—to make it clear that our salvation comes about solely from God's mere generosity—we must be called back to the course of election, those who wish to get rid of all this are obscuring as maliciously as they can what ought to have been gloriously and vociferously proclaimed, and they tear humility up by its very roots. . . .
>
> They who shut the gates that no one may dare seek a taste of this doctrine wrong men no less than God. For neither will anything else suffice to make us humble as we ought to be nor shall we otherwise sincerely feel how much we are obliged to God. . . . He has set forth by his Word the secrets of his will that he has decided to reveal to us. These he decided to reveal in so far as he foresaw that they would concern us and benefit us.[2]

God's glory and our benefit—there Calvin discovered "the usefulness of this doctrine" and "its very sweet fruit."

---

2. *Institutes* 3.21.1 (OS, 4:369f.).

Bibliography

Barth, Karl. *Church Dogmatics*. Translated by Geoffrey W. Bromiley et al. 4 vols. Naperville, Ill.: Allenson, 1936–1969.
———. *Die kirchliche Dogmatik*. 4 vols. Zurich: Evangelischer, 1942.
Barth, Peter. "Calvin." In *Die Religion in Geschichte und Gegenwart*. 2nd ed. 5 vols. Tübingen: Mohr, 1927–1931. 1:1425–37.
———. "*Fünfundzwanzig Jahre Calvinforschung, 1909–1934*." *Theologische Rundschau*, new series, 6 (1934): 161–75, 246–67.
Bauke, Herman. *Die Probleme der Theologie Calvins*. Leipzig: Hinrichs, 1923.
Bavinck, Herman. *Gereformeerde dogmatiek*. 4th ed. 4 vols. Kampen: Kok, 1928–1930.
Berkhof, Louis. *Systematic Theology*. Grand Rapids: Eerdmans, 1953.
Berkouwer, Gerrit C. *Divine Election*. Translated by Hugo Bekker. Grand Rapids: Eerdmans, 1960.
Boettner, Loraine. *The Reformed Doctrine of Predestination*. Grand Rapids: Eerdmans, 1932.
Brunner, H. Emil. *Dogmatics*. Translated by Olive Wyon. 3 vols. Philadelphia: Westminster, 1950–1962.

Calvin, John. *Calvin's Calvinism.* Edited and translated by Henry Cole. Grand Rapids: Eerdmans, 1956.

————. *Commentaries.* Edited and translated by Joseph Haroutunian. Library of Christian Classics, vol. 23. Philadelphia: Westminster, 1958.

————. *Concerning the Eternal Predestination of God.* Translated by J. K. S. Reid. London: Clarke, 1961.

————. *The Epistles of Paul the Apostle to the Galatians, Ephesians, Philippians and Colossians.* Translated by T. H. L. Parker. Grand Rapids: Eerdmans, 1965.

————. *The Epistles of Paul the Apostle to the Romans and to the Thessalonians.* Translated by Ross Mackenzie. Grand Rapids: Eerdmans, 1961.

————. *The Gospel According to St. John and the First Epistle of John.* Translated by T. H. L. Parker. 2 vols. Grand Rapids: Eerdmans, 1959–1961.

————. *Institutes of the Christian Religion.* Edited by John T. McNeill. Translated by Ford Lewis Battles. 2 vols. Library of Christian Classics, vols. 20–21. Philadelphia: Westminster, 1960.

————. *Institution of the Christian Religion . . . 1536.* Translated by Ford Lewis Battles. Atlanta: John Knox, 1975.

————. *Instruction in Faith.* Translated by Paul T. Fuhrmann. Philadelphia: Westminster, 1949.

————. *Letters.* Edited by Jules Bonnet. Translated by David Constable. 2 vols. Edinburgh: Constable, 1855–1857.

————. *Opera quae supersunt omnia.* Edited by Guilielmus Baum, Eduardus Cunitz, and Eduardus Reuss. 59 vols. *Corpus Reformatorum,* vols. 29–87. Brunsvigae: Schwetschke, 1863–1900.

————. *Opera selecta.* Edited by Petrus Barth and Guilielmus Niesel. 5 vols. Munich: Kaiser, 1926–1952.

————. *Sermons on the Epistles of S. Paule to Timothie and Titus.* Translated by L. Tomson. London: Bishop and Woodcoke, 1579.

————. *Theological Treatises.* Edited and translated by J. K. S. Reid. Library of Christian Classics, vol. 22. Philadelphia: Westminster, 1954.

————. *Tracts and Treatises.* Translated by Henry Beveridge. 3 vols. Grand Rapids: Eerdmans, 1958.

Daane, James. *The Freedom of God: A Study of Election and Pulpit.* Grand Rapids: Eerdmans, 1973.

————. "The Principle of Equal Ultimacy of Election and Reprobation." *Reformed Journal,* November 1953, pp. 9–12.

————. *A Theology of Grace.* Grand Rapids: Eerdmans, 1954.

De Jong, Peter Y., ed. *Crisis in the Reformed Churches: Essays in Commemoration of the Great Synod of Dort, 1618–1619.* Grand Rapids: Reformed Fellowship, 1968.

De Klerk, Peter. "Calvin Bibliography 1972." *Calvin Theological Journal* 7 (1972): 221–50.

————. "Calvin Bibliography 1973." *Calvin Theological Journal* 9 (1974): 38–73.

————. "Calvin Bibliography 1974." *Calvin Theological Journal* 9 (1974): 210–40.

————. "Calvin Bibliography 1975." *Calvin Theological Journal* 10 (1975): 175–207.

————. "Calvin Bibliography 1976." *Calvin Theological Journal* 11 (1976): 199–243.

Dowey, Edward A., Jr. "Continental Reformation: Works of General Interest: Studies in Calvin and Calvinism Since 1948." *Church History* 24 (1955): 360–67.

————. *The Knowledge of God in Calvin's Theology.* New York: Columbia University, 1952.

De l'election eternelle de Dieu: Actes du congres international de theologie calviniste, Geneve, 15–18 Juin 1936. Geneva: Labor, 1936.

Engelland, Heinrich. *Gott und Mensch bei Calvin.* Munich: Kaiser, 1934.

Forstman, H. Jackson. *Word and Spirit: Calvin's Doctrine of Biblical Authority.* Stanford: Stanford University, 1962.

Gohler, Alfred. *Calvins Lehre von der Heiligung.* Munich: Kaiser, 1934.

Hauck, Wilhelm-Albert. *Christusglaube und Gottesoffenbarung nach Calvin.* Gütersloh: Bertelsmann, 1939.

————. *Die Erwählten: Prädestination und Heilsgewissheit nach Calvin.* Gütersloh: Bertelsmann, 1950.

————. *Vorsehung und Freiheit nach Calvin.* Gütersloh: Bertels-mann, 1947.

Hunter, A. M. *The Teaching of Calvin.* Westwood, N.J.: Revell, 1950.

Jacobs, Paul, *Prädestination und Verantwortlichkeit bei Calvin.* Neukirchen: Erziehungsvereins, 1937.

Kantzer, Kenneth S. "Calvin and the Holy Scriptures." In *Inspiration and Interpretation,* edited by John F. Walvoord, pp. 115–55. Grand Rapids: Eerdmans, 1957.

Kuiper, Herman. *Calvin on Common Grace.* Grand Rapids: Smitter, 1928.

McNeill, John T. *The History and Character of Calvinism.* New York: Oxford University, 1954.

————. "Thirty Years of Calvin Study." *Church History* 17 (1948): 207–40.

Maury, Pierre. *Predestination and Other Papers.* Translated by Edwin Hudson. Richmond: John Knox, 1957.

Murray, John. *Calvin on Scripture and Divine Sovereignty.* Grand Rapids: Baker, 1960.

————. "The Theology of the Westminster Standards." *The Calvin Forum* 9 (1944): 111–15.

Niesel, Wilhelm. *The Theology of Calvin.* Translated by Harold Knight. Philadelphia: Westminster, 1956.

Otten, Heinz. *Calvins theologische Anschauung von der Prädestination.* Munich: Kaiser, 1938.

Parker, T. H. L. "A Bibliography and Survey of the British Study of Calvin, 1900–1940." *Evangelical Quarterly* 18 (1946): 123–31.

————. *The Doctrine of the Knowledge of God: A Study in the Theology of John Calvin.* Edinburgh: Oliver and Boyd, 1952.

————. *The Oracles of God: An Introduction to the Preaching of John Calvin.* London: Lutterworth, 1947.

Polman, Andries D. R. *De praedestinatieleer van Augustinus, Thomas van Aquino en Calvijn: Een dogmahistorische studie.* Franeker: Wever, 1936.

Quistorp, Heinrich. *Calvin's Doctrine of the Last Things.* Richmond: John Knox, 1955.

Ritschl, Otto. *Dogmengeschichte des Protestantismus.* 4 vols. Leipzig: Hinrichs, 1908–1912; Göttingen: Vandenhoeck and Ruprecht, 1926–1927.

Rückert, Hans. *"Calvin-Literatur seit 1945."* *Archiv für Reformationsgeschichte* 50 (1959): 64–74.

Thornwell, James Henly. *Election and Reprobation.* Columbia: Weir, 1840. Reprinted—Grand Rapids: Baker, 1961.

Torrance, T. F. *Calvin's Doctrine of Man.* Grand Rapids: Eerdmans, 1957.

————. *Kingdom and Church.* Edinburgh: Oliver and Boyd, 1956.

Tylenda, Joseph N. "Calvin Bibliography 1960–1970." *Calvin Theological Journal* 6 (1971): 156–93.

Van Buren, Paul. *Christ in Our Place: The Substitutionary Character of Calvin's Doctrine of Reconciliation.* Grand Rapids: Eerdmans, 1957.

Van Til, Cornelius. *The Defense of the Faith.* Philadelphia: Presbyterian and Reformed, 1955.

————. *The Theology of James Daane.* Philadelphia: Presbyterian and Reformed, 1959.

Wallace, Ronald S. *Calvin's Doctrine of the Word and Sacrament.* Grand Rapids: Eerdmans, 1957.

Warfield, Benjamin B. *Biblical Foundations.* Grand Rapids: Eerdmans, 1958.

————. *Calvin and Calvinism.* New York: Oxford University, 1931.

————. "Predestination in the Reformed Confessions." *The Presbyterian and Reformed Review* 12 (1901): 49–128.

Weber, Hermann. *Die Theologie Calvins: Ihre inner Systematik im Lichte structurpsychologiescher Forschungsmethode.* Berlin: Elsner, 1930.

Weber, Otto. "Calvin." In *Die Religion in Geschichte und Gegenwart.* 3rd ed. 7 vols. Tübingen: Mohr, 1957–1965. 1:1593–99.

Wedenaar, John. "Predestination: An Exposition of Romans 9." Grand Rapids: Baker, n.d. (pamphlet).

Wendel, Francois. *Calvin: The Origins and Development of His Religious Thought.* Translated by Philip Mairet. New York: Harper and Row, 1963.

Zanden, L. Van der. *Praedestinatie: Onze verkiezing in Christus.* Kampen: Kok, 1949.

Author Index

Ambrose, 39
Aquinas, Thomas, 34 n 18, 39
Augustine, 36, 39, 45, 59, 65, 67, 68, 69, 69 n 64, 74, 84, 86

Barth, Karl, 11–12, 15 n 14, 22 n 46, 49 n 95, 51 n 108
Barth, Peter, 11 n 2, 21 n 41
Battles, Ford Lewis, 16 n 16
Bauke, Herman, 78 n 106
Bavinck, Herman, 15 n 12, 16 n 18
Berkhof, Louis, 59 n 16
Berkouwer, Gerrit C., 79 n 109
Bernard of Clairvaux, 44
Beza, Theodorus, 14 n 9

Daane, James, 71 n 74
De Klerk, Peter, 12 n 2, 12 n 7
Dowey, Edward A., Jr., 12 n 2, 21 n 38, 32 n 13, 33 n 15, 34–35 n 19, 52 n 114, 71 n 74, 72 n 79

Hauck, Wilhelm-Albert, 33 n 15, 34 n 18

Jacobs, Paul, 12 n 6, 14 n 10, 16 n 18, 34 n 18, 35 n 19

Jerome, 39

Kantzer, Kenneth S., 21 n 38
Kuiper, Herman, 46 n 73, 84 n 133

McNeill, John T., 11
Murray, John, 21 n 38, 76 n 100

Niesel, Wilhelm, 12 n 4, 12 n 6, 15 n 14, 51 n 108

Origen, 39
Otten, Heinz, 33 n 15

Parker, T. H. L., 11 n 2, 12, 12 n 5
Pighius, Albert, 19, 26, 42, 69–70
Plato, 64
Polman, Andries D. R., 12 n 6, 15 n 15, 16 n 18, 22 n 46, 33 n 15, 55 n 2

Quistorp, Heinrich, 71 n 74

Rückert, Hans, 11 n 2

Sadoleto, Jacopo, 48
Socinus, Laelius, 17 n 19

Scripture Index

Genesis
18:25   65
21:12   36
27:9   37 n 29
48:20   37

Exodus
9:16   80

Job
12:24   23

Psalms   26
chapter 19   82 n 122
103:17   44

Proverbs
16:4   62, 80, 81

Isaiah   83

Jeremiah   83

Ezekiel   83

Malachi
1:2–6   36

Matthew
13:11   83

13:13   83
15:13   50 n 102, 58
24:41   77

Luke
22:32   50 n 102

John
3:16   51
chapter 6   42 n 58
6:37   31 n 3, 42, 50
6:39   31 n 3, 50 n 102, 51
10:27–28   50 n 102
12:39   83
13:18   31, 34 n 19
17:6   53

Acts
13:48   84

Romans   21–22, 25, 29
1:18ff.   82 n 122
5:12ff.   66
8:29–30   43, 81
8:30   44
8:38   50 n 102
chapter 9   16, 22, 26, 38, 39, 56, 61, 62, 79–80, 82 n 119, 83
9:1–5   16 n 17